A WORLD OF DIFFERENCE
THE BIG GREEN POETRY MACHINE

CW00766918

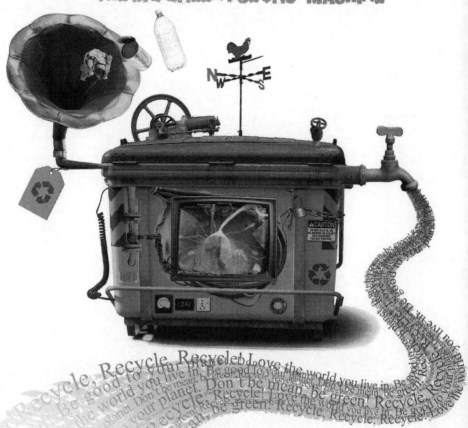

Northern Inspirations
Edited by Vivien Linton

First published in Great Britain in 2009 by:

 Young**Writers**

Young Writers
Remus House
Coltsfoot Drive
Peterborough
PE2 9JX
Telephone: 01733 890066
Website: www.youngwriters.co.uk

All Rights Reserved
Book Design by Ali Smith & Tim Christian
© Copyright Contributors 2008
SB ISBN 978-1-84924-037-6

Foreword

Young Writers' A World of Difference is a showcase for our nation's most brilliant young poets to share their thoughts, hopes and fears for the planet they call home.

Young Writers was established in 1990 to nurture creativity in our children and young adults, to give them an interest in poetry and an outlet to express themselves. Seeing their work in print will encourage them to keep writing as they grow, and become our poets of tomorrow.

Selecting the poems has been challenging and immensely rewarding. The effort and imagination invested by these young writers makes their poems a pleasure to enjoy reading time and time again.

Contents

Oxclose Community School, Washington

Queen Elizabeth High School, Hexham

Ripon Grammar School, Ripon

St Edmund Arrowsmith Catholic High School, Ashton-in-Makerfield

St Joseph's RC Comprehensive School, Hebburn

St Joseph's RC Middle School, Hexham

Teesdale School, Barnard Castle

Whitburn CE School, Whitburn

The Poems

Is This The Future We Created?

Imagine the sky clogged up with a grim shade of deathly black,
Picture the world concealed by a thick sheet of
repugnant debris and rubble,
Bodies smothered by waste,
Young children with bloodshot eyes and cold pale skin shake uncontrollably
and grab anything in sight with desperation.
They scream and scramble away as their own frantic parents turn against
them in madness,
Crowds of delirious people shriek and wail as they swarm and struggle in the
wreckage,
Tumble down buildings once maybe homes torn and crumbled,
Taste pollution and gas as you breathe the thick heavy air,
See no birds or wildlife on the horizon,
Only piles of junk and abandoned skyscrapers
piercing the brownish sky,
Is this the future we created?
Help change it - save the world.

Jessica Eastwood (11)
Allerton Grange High School, Leeds

A Great Thing

The Yorkshire Dales have been a great thing.
A great thing to me.
All my happiest memories
Are in the Dales I see.

But the Yorkshire Dales are changing.
Because of us they're rearranging
Yet we can help through certain ways.
Like when you're on your holidays!

By not dropping litter,
Shutting field gates,
This will help make this region a lot less bitter.

I know it is annoying doing all this.
But with your aid
We could make this country bliss!

Sophie Webster (12)
Andrew Marvell B&E College, Hull

Why?

If I was to *stop*
Go,
Leave this beautiful world.

I would be happy.
I have seen the colours,
I have seen the stars.
There is no other.

Place, time, moment at all.

If black is white,
If wrong is right.
If starving is full,
If life is dull.

We were made specially, individually.
Purposely,

So was the world we live in,
Creatures great and small.

But still my eyes fill with anger,
When I see suffering,
Crying, dying,
Anger.

Join me and together we can change.
Change the way we think,
The way we live,
Look me in the eye and tell me we can.
Make a difference.

Ashleigh Gurnell (11)
Andrew Marvell B&E College, Hull

Planet

Our planet is blue and green
So please help us save all the trees.
Recycle, that's all we need
Please help us save all the greens.

Carmen Medici (11)
Andrew Marvell B&E College, Hull

Green Issues Poem

Come on people, let's recycle,
Get out your car and on to your cycle,
Your cars are letting off lots of pollution,
Come to a decision and make a solution.

Come on people let's recycle.

Why are petrol prices so high?
Hearing lots of people giving off a sigh,
Floods, floods everywhere,
Causing people to despair.

Come on people let's recycle.

Litter, litter everywhere,
People these days do not care.
Why don't people use the bins?
Paper's bad enough, don't mention tins.

Come on people let's recycle.

Get to your lights and turn them off,
Why have them on - they attract moths,
Energy bulbs, energy bulbs, please use them,
All of you should, why not get ten?

Come on people, let's recycle,
Get out of your car and onto your cycle,
Your cars are letting of lots of pollution,
Come to a decision and make a solution.

Danny Broadley (13)
Andrew Marvell B&E College, Hull

No Air

Don't cut down the rainforest
For every tree you cut down
You are preventing the world
From having air
So every time you cut one
Plant two.

Aaron Cartwright (11)
Andrew Marvell B&E College, Hull

3

So Why Are We Killing It?

Help the environment
Think about the world,
Reuse and recycle.

The world is so important
So why are we killing it?
Imagine no world,
So why are we killing it?
We need the world
So why are we killing it?

Help the environment,
Think about the world,
Reuse and recycle.

The environment is polluted
So why are we killing it?
The world is polluted
So why are we killing it?
The universe is polluted
So why are we killing it?

Help the environment,
Think about the world,
Reuse and recycle.

Faye Parrish (12)
Andrew Marvell B&E College, Hull

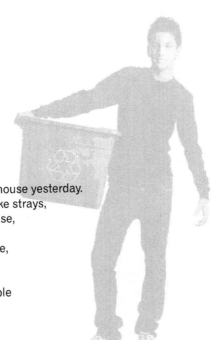

Homeless

We were kicked out of our house yesterday.
Now we are on the street like strays,
Me, my mum and no one else,
Here we are on our own
Nothing to eat, we are alone,
Me and my mum,
All alone
Please help homeless people
Around the world.

Tom Forward (11)
Andrew Marvell B&E College, Hull

Save The World!

Here's something that's easy to do
To save the planet from people like you.
Gases will hang around in the air.
Do you want this to happen - do you even care?
Well listen up because you should
Everyone can stop this, even you could
Litter will soon be draped across the floor.
A flood might come or even a war
Don't leave the light on in the middle of the day
It's broad daylight outside you can see all the same.
Spread the message round and round,
Make a stand, make a sound.
Tell the world, it's going down,
Unless we help to save the town.
Tell everyone this song
Tell them to shout
Listen carefully
Just hear me out
Save energy by walking
Share a car, it starts the talking
Don't leave the telly on
Or the world will be gone.

Hannah Saleh (12)
Andrew Marvell B&E College, Hull

Poem For The World

W e need to help the world.
O ur world in every way.
R apid seas when they used to be calm.
L onely people, who are being harmed.
D isasters happen every day, we will stop them in every way.

P eople dying, suffering so bad.
E ating bad food, they're not glad.
A lways, always going down.
C itizens like that wish to wear a crown.
E verybody come on help, we can stop it with just a touch.

Thomas Hairsine (11)
Andrew Marvell B&E College, Hull

Help The Environment

Pollution is spreading,
More and more everyday
Pollution is spreading,
Help it go away.

You could travel on your bike,
If you are going far
You could travel on your bike,
Instead of driving in a car.

Turn your TV off,
When not in use
Turn your TV off,
And don't make an excuse.

The ice caps are melting
The future's in your hands
The ice caps are melting
In faraway lands.

So help the environment
Don't be a fool,
Help the environment
And stay cool.

Laura Mortimer (12)
Andrew Marvell B&E College, Hull

Green Gases

G o home and turn off your stuff.
R ed lights are a thing of the past,
E nergy saving is the way,
E veryone think of hydrogen fast,
N ow everyone lives today.

G o home and turn off your stuff.
A nd if you litter and think you're rough
S ome coppers will come and give you the cuff
E ven turn to thirty
S een the world? It's really dirty.

Rory Myres (12)
Andrew Marvell B&E College, Hull

Don't Stop The World Going Round!

Here I am walking to school,
Around me there are lots of fools.
Zooming by in their new flash cars,
Fumes galore we will block out the stars.
Don't stop the world going round.

The litter dropped is like dead leaves,
So come on people bin it please.
Bins over here, bins over there,
Don't forget or I will pull out my hair.
Don't stop the world going round.

So come on people take the hint,
Beware and watch your eco-footprint.
Put things in your black bins,
Like cartons, bottles and metal tins.
Don't stop the world going round.

Recycle, reuse all that you use,
Including the wrappers of your own foods.
If we stick together on this case,
We will make the world a better place.
Don't stop the world going round.

Adam Langstaff (12)
Andrew Marvell B&E College, Hull

From You To Us

You give us bright blue skies
We pollute them
You give us clean air
We pollute it
It's our Earth, we live in it and we destroy it
Everybody needs a clean place to live
You give us many kinds of people
We destroy them
You give us countries
We go to war
Help the Big Green Poetry Machine.

Jack Chaytor (11)
Andrew Marvell B&E College, Hull

7

Islands

I stand now upon the bright white sand,
Looking into the lushness of the island.
Birdsong rises to my ear and waves accompany it,
The water swirls around my feet.

Now I stand in a lush rainforest,
Birds, trees and animals surround me.
The sound of falling trees and fleeing creatures,
Drowns the beauty and crushes the environment.

Here I stand in countryside wide,
Farming covers the land.
Then suddenly houses arise,
Upon the hilltops high.

A sprawling metropolis is where I stand,
Trucks and cars pollute the air.
Insects and birds cannot be heard,
Against the manmade world.

The heat of Israel is where I stand,
Amongst the homeless,
What would happen if I went back to the island?

Sam Carmichael (11)
Andrew Marvell B&E College, Hull

Green

G o green and help save the world for tomorrow, we
R eally need you to help save the world.
E nvironments are changing, animals are dying.
E verybody can help by recycling some of their rubbish.
N ow we can make a difference by using less energy.

I ssues are habitats, homes, animals and more,
S o we need to help and save them all.
S olar energy is being introduced, we can use less clothes washes,
U se the car for only long journeys and walk for shorter.
E verybody can help save the world,
S o make a difference today and make the world better tomorrow.

Liam Brookes (12)
Andrew Marvell B&E College, Hull

8

Fighting For Freedom

I wake up and all I see,
Are dead bodies beside me.
I stare around in fear and fright,
I can see that dark stormy night.
I look down at my gun, hard,
I can imagine myself in that graveyard.

I turn around
As I see a man hit the ground
I look round to see what I can see
And there stands my enemy looking straight at me.
All I know is that he is in pain.
I wish this was a PlayStation game.

All I can hear is screaming and crying
They say war is glory, they are lying
The booming bombs, the shooting of the guns
I wish I could go home and see my sons.

I feel close to death
Could this be my last breath?

Lauren Cartlidge, Rebecca Cartlidge & Laura Kitching (13)
Andrew Marvell B&E College, Hull

Abandoned

It was there in the corner of an alley
Huddled, hungry and homeless
Scrimping and scraping for the littlest scrap
Going out of its mind
Running around in circles
In the bins sheltering from rain
Which could freeze it to death
Kicked out of the house
The loss of hair will never grow back

This is one of millions of unlucky dogs or
Cats abandoned from their home.

What will you do?

Matthew Sumpton (13)
Andrew Marvell B&E College, Hull

Imagine

Imagine
You're in a place
With blue sea and beautiful sandy beaches
Imagine
What it would feel like
Sunbathing on a beach
Like that
The sun blazing down on you
The peaceful feeling that you would get
But imagine
What it would be like
If people started to litter it
The sea would have rubbish in
Cigarette butts would be dug in the sand
It would be an awful place to sunbathe
So we need to protect it
So we can have a gorgeous place to go
Help us enjoy it
Not destroy it!

Leah Dearing (12)
Andrew Marvell B&E College, Hull

What Happens Next?

We live in a country where no one cares
They do what they want without being scared
But one day all that will change
But then it will be too late
It will all be very strange.
The animals gone
Islands are flooded.

We could stop this and it could go away
If you live the right way
Don't throw rubbish
Or waste electricity,
You know what will happen!
Think about our world.

Rebecca Casey (12)
Andrew Marvell B&E College, Hull

10

In This City

From the quiet countryside of Yorkshire
To the heaving traffic of New York
From the mansions of Beverly Hills
To the slums of Sao Paulo
Our Earth is great
With fascinating animals
And the natural sculptures
Our Earth is the best
But this will not go on forever
With the climate change
Animals will go extinct
And the sculptures will fade away
We don't want to grow up in a polluted world
So why don't we change?
Why don't we recycle?
Why don't we turn the TV *off?*
Why don't we get insulation to save energy?
Why do we cut down trees?
Why don't we save the world?

Curtis Grundy (11)
Andrew Marvell B&E College, Hull

Global Warming

G lobal warming is coming.
L et's stop using cars and start walking.
O ur whole world could be destroyed.
B ut the world's authorities don't care.
A ll the polar bears are dying.
L ots of icebergs are melting.

W e need to put a stop to it.
A ll the Polar regions' species are becoming extinct.
R eally people think it's OK.
M ight it all be stopped one day?
I ce is becoming water.
N o we can't ignore it!
G o and stop global warming.

Jake Scott (11)
Andrew Marvell B&E College, Hull

Environment

Environment, what can I say?
We can write about this any day.
But Miss is making us, so now I'll write,
About environment day and night.

In the forest trees are getting sawed,
Big dints in them like they've been gnawed.
Humans don't understand,
What they're doing to this beautiful land.

Scorpions, toads, creatures in the sand,
These are found in the desert land,
In the day it's quiet
But in the night it comes alive.
Rain, rain, go away,
That's not what the toad would say
Come on rain hurry up
So I can suck you up like a cup
He expresses,
Just waiting in all the sandy messes.

Alex Ross (12)
Andrew Marvell B&E College, Hull

Ice Caps

The ice caps are melting
They are melting fast
The ice caps are melting
The polar bears won't last.

The ice caps are melting
Help your future now
The ice caps are melting
Do you know how?

Go on your bike or the train
Instead of using the aeroplane
So now you know what to do
A better future for me and for you.

Lauren Carter (13)
Andrew Marvell B&E College, Hull

12

Canary Islands

The sun blazes down,
Brightly all around,
Upon the peaceful waves,
Lighting up once-dark caves,
Exotic wildlife lives in the forest,
But some have been wrecked by careless tourists,
The beautiful fish in the sea are a wonder to watch for me.

The sky is always blue,
The beach is too beautiful to be true,
But it has been eroded away,
So it will have to end one day,
The beach is a good tourist attraction,
But may end in a bad reaction,
As the beautiful beach is plagued by litter which causes pollution,
At the moment we have no solution,
So as beautiful as the island may be,
It has lots of problems so we'll have to see.

Lewis Bower (11)
Andrew Marvell B&E College, Hull

Questions All Around

No food, no water, no shelter and no heat,
Children crying - they have nothing to eat.
Parents working for pennies and crumbs,
Going home to a family huddled in the slums.
Does the world care?
Is it enough?
Do the lives of these people have to be so tough?
Look around here, see happiness and smiles,
Then look at the sadness across the miles.
What can we do to make their lives good?
Can we send extra help, and presents, and food?
Can we help them learn how to harvest their land?
And give them all a helping hand?
It's our world, our life and now we should see,
That there is no need for such poverty.

Victoria Wilkinson (12)
Andrew Marvell B&E College, Hull

Recycling Song

Recycle, recycle
Yeah you got to recycle
Don't throw your bottles away
Try to recycle every day
People who throw things away
Go to the dump and see what's there today
Try to recycle every day
While your dad is drinking beer
Sometimes he asks, 'Can you throw that away dear?'
She always says, 'No!'
So try to recycle every day.
From the top!
Recycle, recycle
Yeah you got to recycle
Don't throw your bottles away
Try to recycle every day.

Try to recycle!

Olivia Shepherdson (11)
Andrew Marvell B&E College, Hull

Be Green!

'Why should I recycle?' you say
Well each minute and hour of every day
The Earth's being destroyed by the pollution of cars,
One day we will need to live on Mars.
Ice caps are melting by the warmth of the sun.
Cities are flooding, soon there will be nowhere to run.
But you can change that by being eco-friendly.
And by that I mean being more green.
Recycling, composting, come on, don't be mean.
So if one day you're wondering,
How can I save this place?
Think, be green!
And clear up the disgrace.
Be green!

Kayleigh Scott (13)
Andrew Marvell B&E College, Hull

Green Life

The cars won't be running,
If the petrol costs too much,
We all want a green life.

If the landfills get too big,
There won't be room for
The important things,
We all want a green life.

If you want a polluted neighbourhood,
Then carry on the way you are,
Because every little thing
We do has an effect on the world,
We all want a green life.

We all want to breathe fresh air
But pollution is all around,
Left and right up and down
We all have a green life.

Chloe Batty (12)
Andrew Marvell B&E College, Hull

Green Issues Poem

Petrol prices, petrol prices sky high
If I said they were cheap, I would be telling a lie.
People, people, littering, pollution,
Let's make a stop with a solution.
Travelling, travelling, don't go in the car
Travel on a bike, it isn't that far.
Floods, floods, they destroy anything in their way,
Let's try to stop them, even if we have to pay.
Recycle, recycle that's the thing to do,
Make the Earth greener and us too.
Air travel, air travel, don't go high,
Be a grounds man and just walk by.
Green issues, green issues everywhere we see
Let's take care of our environment, until it's a better place to be!

Callum Grima (12)
Andrew Marvell B&E College, Hull

Global Warming Has Begun . . .

Global warming has begun,
It isn't going to be fun,
It's a war that cannot be won,
And it's only just begun . . .

The floods are here,
We'd better stay clear,
Or else live in fear,
Global warming has begun.

Pollution is in the air,
If only we'd taken care,
We should have been aware,
Global warming has begun.

If we become more keen,
At becoming green,
The Earth will be clean,
Global warming will be gone.

Laura Cross (13)
Andrew Marvell B&E College, Hull

What Will Happen?

What will happen?
In 50 years where will we be?
No animals there will be
Everyone travelling in their cars
Even if they don't have to go far.

All the pollution in the air
Because no one now cares
If people could just recycle
It could turn into a car or bicycle.

The North Pole will be bare
Without the polar bears.
With all this pollution
You're our only solution.

Claire McPherson (12)
Andrew Marvell B&E College, Hull

16

Our Environment

The beaming sun glowing,
A nice breeze blowing,
Hot blue water flowing,
Warm sand covering the land.

Is what we want!
Not this!

Don't let animals' homes disappear,
Let more appear,
Trees are living too,
What have they done to you?
Help save animals and plants.

Don't drop litter,
It makes our streets a critter,
Put rubbish in bins,
Even tins,
It makes our lives easier!

Hannah Rusling (11)
Andrew Marvell B&E College, Hull

Littering!

Rubbish to the left,
Rubbish to the right,
Dog poo in the middle,
Chewy on my shoe,
So much rubbish every day,
If they're caught they will pay,
So many rats, let's scream,
Please, keep our planet clean!
So next time think when you litter,
Or you'll pay,
So don't drop any more litter,
Or we'll be very bitter.

Chris Taylor (11)
Andrew Marvell B&E College, Hull

All Around The World

All around the world is wide,
Under, over, side to side
I am ever so proud of what I own
The whole world in my hands, it is my home
From ants to whales
From rain to gales
Nature's gifts, like waves and mountains
Manmade things, houses and fountains
Sandy beaches, ever so calm
Under the rock, there sits a clam
In the city the story's not the same
It is a completely different game,
All the smoke, all the cars,
The steamy air, the chocolate bars
The skyscrapers built as high as can see,
As I look at the sky, what else could there be?

Anastasiia Khrypunova (12)
Andrew Marvell B&E College, Hull

Please Recycle

Save our land
Don't expand
The amount of rubbish
It would smell really bad
And it will be very sad
Please recycle
It is unfair
Take some care
Why don't you reuse?
You can recreate
So come on mate
Save our world.

Matthew Howe (11)
Andrew Marvell B&E College, Hull

The World

The flowers bloom in the shining sun,
The sea crashes onto the sand as if it is horses,
There are children laughing and having fun.

Rubbish crunches under your feet,
Every drop of water is danger,
The children shake on their seats.

The snow drifts gently to the ground,
Polar bears swim gracefully through the ocean,
Penguins waddle through the snow,
And the cold winter air whistles through my ears.

Abbie Carmichael (11)
Andrew Marvell B&E College, Hull

Recycle!

Green is good,
Recycling is what we do,
Paper,
Plastic,
Cardboard,
And plant cuttings too.
Stick them in the bin,
Then wheel it back outside,
Wait until it decomposes,
Then start it all again next time!

Jennifer Hepworth (11)
Andrew Marvell B&E College, Hull

Life

Rainforests rolling over the hills unhindered?
I think not, trees chopped down turned to paper, axes chop, chainsaws roar,
To them it's all the same, while at the moment a thousand miles away
Two opposing armies battle in vain
Because while both kill and maim neither one wins the game
And all the while the celebrities grow in fame
Why?
It's just insane and it's such a shame
Those human desires have not been tamed.

Arron Poucher (12)
Andrew Marvell B&E College, Hull

Be Green

Everybody lets off all sorts of pollutions,
All those scientists say they've got the solutions.
But are they real or just fake?
For all we know they're dragging oil out a lake,
Cycle, cycle get out of your car,
Take your bike if it isn't far,
Help us, turn your washes to 30°,
Save some energy, you won't get dirty,
Be green!

Kurtis Hazel (12)
Andrew Marvell B&E College, Hull

Pollution Poem

The sky was blue
Now it's grey
It does not change it does not go away
The sea was calm, now it's rough
Riding the sea has never been so tough
The air is bad, it's not clear, it's damaging
The world and its atmosphere.

Richard Inglis (11)
Andrew Marvell B&E College, Hull

Big Green

B e kind to the planet
I n the bin your rubbish goes
G reen is what the Earth should be

G reen is what our future is
R efrain from pollution
E arth should stay green
E arth should stay clean
N ow is the time to do your part.

Aimee Wadsworth & Shannon Sirrs (11)
Andrew Marvell B&E College, Hull

Think Of . . .

Think of the clear blue water.
Think of the smooth golden sand.
Think of the warmth shining down on to you.
Think of the fun you would have.

Think of the muddy polluted water.
Think of the littered sand.
Think of the sun not being in your direction.
Think of the worst time you could ever have on holiday!

Shaunna Bennett (11)
Andrew Marvell B&E College, Hull

My Pollution In The Environment

The seas are dull in Hull
Pollution is everywhere
They just don't care
They throw their rubbish everywhere
Trampy beaches will kill the animals
Seas are grey and dull
Why is the pollution turned to a matter
This environment is no good.

Craig Wilkinson (11)
Andrew Marvell B&E College, Hull

Don't Kill The World - Save The World

Don't kill the world - save the world,
Recycle what you can!
Turn off what you're not using,
Be environmentally friendly
Only use what you need,
Reuse things
Don't kill the world - save the world,
Recycle what you can.

Gemma Maslin (12)
Andrew Marvell B&E College, Hull

Extinction

Endangered animals like the white lion
Soon they'll be dead and we'll be cryin'
Even though they'll be dead
You poachers cut off their heads.
The bald eagle will soon die
No one in the world shall comply
Even poachers don't care
The bald eagles soar through the air.

Mark Boynton (12)
Andrew Marvell B&E College, Hull

Protect Our World

Protect our world,
Save the planet,
Recycle your rubbish,
Recycle your trash,
Protect our world,
Save the planet,
You can do it,
I know you can.

Daniel Pridgeon (11)
Andrew Marvell B&E College, Hull

Litter

L itter, keep it off the floor
I n the bin it goes
T he bins are there so put it in
T hen the litter stays off the floor
E veryone stop throwing litter onto the ground and start throwing it
into the bin
R ecycle your rubbish and make it into something else.

Angel Bidwell (11)
Andrew Marvell B&E College, Hull

Going Green

People think that they're going green but they're not at all.
They think switching lights off now and then will make a difference,
But it doesn't.
We need to make long term changes like stop using ferries
and aeroplanes.
If we carry on like this we will destroy our planet,
Melt the ice caps and we'll be living in the dark.

Marvin Lee (13)
Andrew Marvell B&E College, Hull

Our Earth

Our Earth is precious
We'll have nowhere to go if our Earth's going down
And pollution is going up,
So do something good
Go green, put your rubbish in the bin,
Help save our Earth!

Georgia Tomlinson (11)
Andrew Marvell B&E College, Hull

Eco, Eco, Eco

G reen, green, grass is no more
O xygen will be gone

E missions from cars
C ongests the world
O ur precious Earth will be gone.

Megan Gallagher (11)
Andrew Marvell B&E College, Hull

Pollution Poem

What are we doing?
What is happening?
Could you answer my questions?
Why not walk a few times a week, you could lose some weight.
There used to be summers
There used to be winters
What has happened?
I need to know!

The ice is melting
The water levels are rising
In a few hundred years
Our countries will be under
When it comes to the world the animals will get the slaughter
So what are we going to do?
So if you don't help, we are coming for you!

Please stop doing it
Protect the ozone layer
Protect us from the sun
So we can have some fun
We could wake up in the morning and go outside with lots of great pride!

We can do it you know you can
Do your part
And help the world's heart
And stop it from dying later on!

Jack Cheetham (12)
Burscough Priory Science College, Burscough

To Save Energy

The Earth is going to die
That is not a lie
You've really got to try
To save energy.

Put your cans in the tin
Put your paper in the bin
Do loads of recycling
To save energy.

Put your lights out
When you are not about
There is no doubt
This saves energy.

Saving trees is good
Use more soft wood
Please try, you really should
To save energy.

The Earth is going to die
That is not a lie
You've really got to try
To save energy.

Jake Higham (12)
Burscough Priory Science College, Burscough

Environment

I woke up one morning, everything was fine
I woke up the next day and the streets were messy.
I looked in the field there were lots of trees,
I looked the next day they were all gone.
I was on my way to school I could see the blue sky
I look the next day all I could see was fumes!
I was on the way back, I could see the street.
I turned around and looked again, all I could see was chewy.

Sam Morton (12)
Burscough Priory Science College, Burscough

We Are The Solution

Climate change,
Climate change is bad.
There is no one else to blame
So don't be lame
Climate change is serious
So don't be delirious
We are the solution.

Climate change,
The ozone layer is gonna burn,
Then you will learn,
We need to stop pollution,
We are the solution.

Climate change,
We're killing the Earth,
And all it's worth.
We can't wait,
Soon it will be too late,
We need to work together,
Before we destroy the Earth together,
We are the solution.

Nicola Brandwood (12)
Burscough Priory Science College, Burscough

Won't We Ever Learn?

Why do we leave the telly on standby,
Will it hurt to turn it off?

Why do we dig big holes in the ground and fill them with depleted uranium
and rubbish?

Can't you see it's us who are melting the ice caps and it's us that floods the
world?

Can't you see it will be too late and the world won't be here by the time we
realise?
Think
Won't you ever learn?

Tristan Oldroyd (12)
Burscough Priory Science College, Burscough

Recycle, Renew, Reuse

Recycle, renew, reuse
The three Rs
They help us to give
Nature a helping hand
To save the planet.
Recycle
Plastic bottles
Bottles, boots,
Boots and clothes
Clothes and shoes
Recycle these and do your bit
Renew
Clothes, leather, butter boxes
Boxes and cardboard boxes and chairs
Chairs and beds and glass, renew these and do your bit
Reuse
Clothes, leather and boxes
Boxes, chairs and beds
Reuse, recycle, renew
Help to save the planet.

Genevieve Hales (12)
Burscough Priory Science College, Burscough

Save The World

We blame other people, why?
Nothing can stop what we've done to the Earth
Or can it? Stop, stop, please.
The cars we make are killing the Earth,
The oil we use too, stop it, stop it.
Why can't we use water?
We know we can use it, use it please
We're doing nothing to help the Earth, why, why don't we stop?
Every single second we live, the Earth is dying.
Why don't we stop killing the Earth?
We can help it and save ourselves,
Stop, stop, we can help the planet.

Ross Ingram (13)
Burscough Priory Science College, Burscough

World Change

The air is clean,
The seasons are real
The cheep of the wild
It makes me smile.

The extreme weather
The carbon foot
The climate change
That litterbug.

That natural feeling
Them gases gone,
The friends of Earth
Are back again.

That warm summer sun,
The cold winter night,
Just to show us all,
To hold the world tight.

Alexa Cross (13)
Burscough Priory Science College, Burscough

I'm Stuck In Traffic

I'm stuck in traffic
I hate the noise
Beep, beep
I can smell the fumes
Through the open window
Help, the world is choking
On the car fumes, as am I
I can feel the seat
So soft, so nice,
Go away nasty noise
And don't come back.

Nathan Walsh (12)
Burscough Priory Science College, Burscough

Pollution

All around the world
People don't know about
Global warming, the greenhouse effect and more,
Just think about it.

All the cars big, small, white and black,
The smoke is sickening!
It's killing us all.
Just think about it.

Evil men chop down trees,
Not knowing that they're killing us.
Destroying our air supply!
Just think about it.

Polluted rivers, factories, litter and more,
That is what's wrong today.
Just open your eyes and look,
Just think about it.

Carly Steele (12)
Burscough Priory Science College, Burscough

I'm An Iceberg!

I was big, powerful and strong
And I looked over everything
And I was like an island, so long.

The sun was getting hotter
And I was shrinking and getting small but,
There is nothing I can do.

The waves were drowning me
And pushing me along
I was losing my strength
And now I am not so strong.

The fish,
The seals,
The penguins,
And the whales
Need me but I'm slowly
Melting away . . .

Heather Watson (13)
Burscough Priory Science College, Burscough

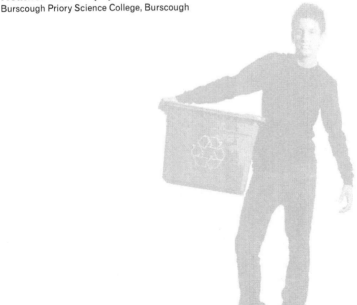

Why?

Why can I see rivers that are green, not blue?
Why can I see lights turned on in daylight?
Why can I see grey clouds?
Why can I see people using cars?
Why can I see landfill sites?
Why can I see animals suffering?

Why can I hear only a few birds singing?
Why can I hear car engines?
Why can't I hear footsteps?
Why can't I hear the clanking chain of a bike?

Why can I smell the burning of bacon which will have to be cooked again?
Why can I smell the burning of rubber?
Why can I smell the car engines?
Why doesn't everyone recycle?
Why?

Danielle Hayman (12)
Burscough Priory Science College, Burscough

War

They are fighting for their country,
To let us all be free,
Some of them lose their lives,
Just for you and me,
Some of them are young,
Some of them are old,
Some of them have hair,
And some are bald.
Their families are waiting nervously,
To see them marching in,
They just want to see their faces,
And make a massive din.
They need a lot of support,
To help them keep on going,
No matter where you are,
Your help should keep on showing.

Rebekah Foulds (12)
Cardinal Allen Catholic High School, Fleetwood

Climate Change

C ycle to school or work.
L ook after the ice caps before they are gone.
I n the car don't rev your engine.
M ake a difference.
A car ride, no way!
T urn your washing machines to 30°
E njoy the environment.

C hange will happen
H elp before it's too late
A nd the sea rises to melt the ice
N o one out there to help
G ive polar bears an opportunity
E verything needs a chance.

Lauren Warburton (11)
Cardinal Allen Catholic High School, Fleetwood

A Letter For Climate Change

C ome on, save the world.
L et the world stay here for longer.
I ce caps are melting.
M ake the polar bears live longer.
A ll we can do is reduce and recycle.
T ell the world to save the planet.
E arth will be drowned in water.

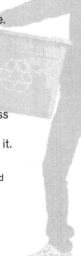

C ome on, it's not a lot.
H ills of flowers and grass
A nd will this last and
N ot to forget the rabbits in the grass
G o on, save us *before it's too late*
E arth will be saved if we look after it.

David Whitaker (11)
Cardinal Allen Catholic High School, Fleetwood

The War

Fighting through the muddy dirt of the Earth
Huffing and puffing and hurt,
Gasping for breath as they ran through the mud.

Dodging the bombs from above, hurt and some dead,
But no one to their aid,
Hoping and hoping they would be saved.

Knowing their time had come to an end
They were fighting for our country
Pay it some respect,
Because most of those men are now dead.
They were strong and brave.

So just be happy and thankful for what they gave.

Hanya Morcos (12)
Cardinal Allen Catholic High School, Fleetwood

Untitled

She lies crying in her room all alone.
She does this every day when she gets home
I wonder what could it be that could make such a young girl cry.
That she wishes she could die.
She goes to school but is too frightened to learn.
The problem was the other kids at school
Who hit her and call her a fool
She has no friends and nowhere to turn.
All she needs is just one friend.
Someone to talk to help the misery end.
Do you sit next to her?
Would you offer her your hand in friendship
Or are you just a bully too?

Katie Williams (13)
Cardinal Allen Catholic High School, Fleetwood

War, Homeless And Climate Change

War is destroying the world.
After we will have to build.
Hopefully it will stop soon.
At noon or under the moon.

When you have no home.
You will start to moan.
You may start to get ill.
Or wish for a magic pill.

Polar bears are losing their ice.
Which isn't very nice.
They will soon start to die.
Before we have time to say bye.

Matty Keel (12)
Cardinal Allen Catholic High School, Fleetwood

My Mixed Poem

We should live in peace
People are dying too soon
It has to stop
People should have homes
Too many people on the streets
The streets are dirty
Animals should be alive
They are becoming extinct
People should not kill animals
Litter should be put in a bin
Animals get killed when people litter.
Litter is a dirty thing.

Bethany Smith (11)
Cardinal Allen Catholic High School, Fleetwood

Environment

E veryone's dream is for a better world.
N o one cares! Throwing litter, being racist and all the wars.
V iolence is just killing the Earth, trees and animals.
I wish people would recycle,
R ainforests are being destroyed
O ceans are dirty, full of rubbish
N ot always do animals live when they are being polluted
M ore and more trees are being cut down (*reuse paper please!*)
E nvironment is a great place as long as we respect it!
N ow help the Earth, animals and trees
T ogether we can help!

Lloyd Thomas (11)
Cardinal Allen Catholic High School, Fleetwood

Acrostic Poem About Rainforests

R ainforests are being chopped down
A nimals are being killed
I n the future some children will not know what a panda is.
N ature is dying away
F rogs' habitats are rainforests and lakes in rainforests
O ceans are full of oil
R ubbish shall go in the bin, not on the floor
E lectric is making carbon dioxide
S ome animals will be extinct by 2017
T rees make our oxygen and people are chopping the down.
S ome animals are very rare.

Danielle Watson (11)
Cardinal Allen Catholic High School, Fleetwood

War Acrostic Haiku

W ar is everywhere
A lways in the world today
R emember them all.

Courtney Hadgraft (11)
Cardinal Allen Catholic High School, Fleetwood

War

In the war some people died
Some ran away and went to hide
That's what I said some people hid
It was worse for you if you were a kid.
Some people shot
Some people stabbed
Some people tortured
Some people gagged.
So that's the story of the war
All I say is, *'No more!'*

Bradley Ashton (12)
Cardinal Allen Catholic High School, Fleetwood

War And Racism

W orldwide decisions made and rejected
A rguments go further
R eady the missiles, fire!

R acial discrimination
A fghanistan
C ausing a lot of offence
I nternational
S abotage
M ore racism = more war.

Steven Boyce (12)
Cardinal Allen Catholic High School, Fleetwood

Recycling

R emove all rubbish!
E arth will be destroyed.
C ling to the edge of the Earth.
Y es it's not too late.
C an you recycle for your own sake?
L itter lying on the ground.
I don't want to die, do you?
N agging all day.
G o on, recycle any litter you see!

Dominic Griffiths (12)
Cardinal Allen Catholic High School, Fleetwood

Recycling Acrostic Poem

R espect the environment
E nd the pollution
C limate change must stop
Y ou are responsible
C arry on reusing
L itter belongs in a recycling bin
I am giving a warning before it's too late
N ever bin, recycle
G ive to the planet and play your part.

Sophie Quigley (12)
Cardinal Allen Catholic High School, Fleetwood

Recycle, Recycle

R ecycling is good not bad,
E verything cannot be recycled.
C ardboard, paper and even a shoe.
Y ou can do something too,
C an you put stuff in the right bin?
L ove the planet and other people might too
E ven you can change the world if you try too!

Anneka Vink (12)
Cardinal Allen Catholic High School, Fleetwood

The World Is Dying

The smoke in the air
People don't think it's fair
It's killing the world
It's getting cold
Everything is turning into mould
It's killing the world
The flowers bloom
Then die the next day
The world is dying.

Abigail Sieradzki (11)
Cardinal Allen Catholic High School, Fleetwood

War

They're fighting for their country,
Iraq, Afghanistan,
Some die for their family,
Some fight in Pakistan.
They fight until they die,
Or maybe they shall live,
They're fighting for their country,
We hope that they will live.

Freya Joensen (11)
Cardinal Allen Catholic High School, Fleetwood

Poverty People

It's time to come home for tea
There is nothing on the table for me.
I sit there crying, moaning and whining,
Because I only earn sixty five pence.
It you could give a pound a week
You could stop me being so weak.
Thanks to groups like Oxfam and CAFOD
They keep us on our feet.

Shawn Thomas (12)
Cardinal Allen Catholic High School, Fleetwood

38

Recycle

R euse, reduce, recycle
E lectric bills should go down
C ans on the street
Y es it's bad
C ardboard in gardens
L itter on the street
E nergy is being wasted.

Aiden Whelan (11)
Cardinal Allen Catholic High School, Fleetwood

Slaughter Must Stop!

Set the animals free of captivity
Slaughter is a no-no to me
Every year a lot of animals are killed
And one day your favourite animal may be extinct
But you can help by giving a little donation every month
Together we can stop slaughter of animals!
You are their only hope.

Tara Johnson (11)
Cardinal Allen Catholic High School, Fleetwood

Animals

A nimals are kind to the environment
N ever eat animals
I think some animals are cute
M any animals are herbivores
A ll animals have different scents
L arge animals are funny
S ome animals are smelly.

Thomas Cressey (12)
Cardinal Allen Catholic High School, Fleetwood

I Don't Want

I don't want to be in a world where animals can't be free.
I don't want to be in a world where it destroys it all for you and me.
I don't want to be in a world where pollution hurts it all.
I don't want to be in a world where all the homeless stumble and fall.
I've listed all the things that make me sad.
I want more things to make me glad
To be alive.

Daniel Whyte (12)
Cardinal Allen Catholic High School, Fleetwood

Recycle

R is for recycling litter . . .
E is for energy . . .
C is for clean streets.
Y is for you should clean your bit.
C is for cleaning the environment.
L is for litter.
E is for eco-schools.

Jack Hayton (11) & Callum Moran (12)
Cardinal Allen Catholic High School, Fleetwood

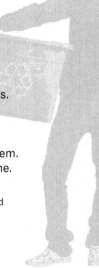

Animals In Danger

A nimals are becoming extinct.
N ot many animals in poor countries.
I would like to save the animals.
M any are losing their homes.
A nimals need to be saved.
L itter pollutes animals and kills them.
S ome animals have no proper home.

Charlotte Beighton (11)
Cardinal Allen Catholic High School, Fleetwood

Animal Life

A nd don't chop down trees.
N ever be cruel to animals.
I guanas are one of them needing help.
M onkeys are as well.
A nd don't hunt animals.
L ovely little animals.
S ad because you're destroying their habitat.

Daniel Mageean (11)
Cardinal Allen Catholic High School, Fleetwood

Pearl Harbour

They leave a trail of disaster
But it isn't very fair
To the people that are homeless
The Japanese who bombed by air
The ships that sank the people
That died it is a day to remember.

Kieran Cole (11)
Cardinal Allen Catholic High School, Fleetwood

Litter

L itter = bin
I don't like litter,
T oday people still drop litter even though you get fined.
T ry to put it in a bin
E veryone is littering
R ubbish everywhere!

Katie Wright (11)
Cardinal Allen Catholic High School, Fleetwood

Racism

R acism is a thing of the bad books
A nd can cause trouble worldwide!
C areful what you say!
I t's not nice to call names
S o remember it can disturb people and break their hearts.
M aybe we could stop it, but we need your help!

Mark Nesbitt (12)
Cardinal Allen Catholic High School, Fleetwood

Extinction

Look at the polar bear it's fur so white
It's like a giant glimmer of light
But some people are filled with spite
And don't think they're a beautiful sight,
So get out of the car and wish upon a star,
For that star could carry a dream so far.

Senga Roberts (11)
Cardinal Allen Catholic High School, Fleetwood

Racism

R is for racism
A ll people should be equal
C an you stop it?
I t doesn't matter, black or white?
S o try to help!
M ake it stop!

Sarah Moran (11)
Cardinal Allen Catholic High School, Fleetwood

Letters For Litter

L   is for letting the world change
I   is for ignoring the world
T   is for tatty world
T   is for tidy up
E   is for extinction of animals.
R   is for realising that the world is changing.

Victoria Thomas (12)
Cardinal Allen Catholic High School, Fleetwood

Litter

L   itter is horrible
I   t smells, it's dirty
T   ogether we can stop litter
T   oday, tomorrow,
E   veryone needs to help out
R   ecycle litter.

Lauren Overing (11)
Cardinal Allen Catholic High School, Fleetwood

Litter

L   itter is ruining our world!
I   can't do anything about it!
T   ogether we can make it stop!
T   ogether we can save the world!
E   veryone needs to help!
R   ight here, right now!

Sam Willan (11)
Cardinal Allen Catholic High School, Fleetwood

Racism, Please Stop

R eally does not matter what colour you are.
A nd it is what is inside that counts
C olour is not important
I don't mind, do you?
S kin is just an outside.
M any people do it and I bet you have too.

Ellena Brown (11)
Cardinal Allen Catholic High School, Fleetwood

Garbage World

L itter is bad for the environment
I t will make streets smell
T he world is turning into garbage
T here is a way to stop it
E veryone should . . .
R ecycle.

Joshua Cody (11)
Cardinal Allen Catholic High School, Fleetwood

A Few Little Words

While we sit around all day
It's the planet Earth that has to pay
Toxic fumes and needless waste
Leave our whole planet defaced.

A cry for help from the lower classes
A cry in vain for the masses
The world is controlled by the wealthy
But not all the people in this world are healthy.

War is a vulture perched high above
Swooping down on the peaceful dove
Fighting through bomb and shell
We've made our own manmade Hell.

Drunken murderers wander our streets
With bottles of cider at their feet
Knife attacks happen all the time
All over the world it is a crime.

Earthquakes, hurricanes, no food or water
Fearing for our sons and daughters
Fire and waves threaten them all
Our society just waiting to tell.

But a few little words won't save the world.

Alex Lori (14)
Cottingham High School, Cottingham

Our World

It's our world in which we live.
It's our choice what we do.
If you just put rubbish in the bin.
What will other people think of you?

Maybe if we recycle it.
Will that make a difference in any way?
Why can't we just do our bit
To help us bring another day.

Emily Hodgson (12)
Longfield School, Darlington

The Changing World

When the last star has fallen
Another child dies
Just see the sadness standing there
Bleeding through their eyes.

No money for education,
No money for medicines,
They are starting to take drugs,
So please give them a chance.

And now as well as taking drugs,
They are into dealing.
All of them are doing this
To hide all their feelings.

Help us to look after them
And make their dreams come true
We need your help with this
It's all down to you.

There are children all over this world,
That need a loving home.
Please can you help them,
Because they need your love.

They struggle for survival,
They work all day and night.
But they also stick together,
To get through their life.

Most of them are now into drugs,
And smoking cigarettes.
But all of them are now drinking
To drown their sorrow and regrets.

Now about World War II,
When Hitler was the man.
Whenever the German army came,
Everyone just ran.

But all of them that did fight,
Are now known as heroes.
But whenever they were fighting,
Hitler made them feel like zeros.

Now that everything's changed,
The world's not as close.
Now people are dying,
With blood as red as rose.

Lauren Bovill (13)
Longfield School, Darlington

Help

Drip, drip, drop,
Goes the water in the bath
Wasting water is not a laugh,
People need it,
People use it
People drink it,
But don't waste it.

Bin, bin, bin,
Goes the food in the bin,
Wasting food is not a win,
People eat it,
People bin it,
Bin's not the word to win it.

Just help,
And help,
And stop these people from a yelp,
Let's help the poor,
And stop the fear,
People need us,
To give them what they need,
Water to drink,
But food to eat,
Just please help these people today!

Samantha Trainor (12)
Longfield School, Darlington

Oh No! Ozone

Greenhouse gases,
Factories here and there,
What's so good about polluting the air?

Landfill sites,
Litter on the streets,
What's so difficult in keeping things neat?

Sea levels rising,
Ice caps melting,
Could this be the cause of all the flooding?

Endangered animals,
Tigers, pandas, bears,
Why keep doing it, does nobody care?

Newspapers here,
Plastic bottles there,
Shouldn't we recycle, do you think it's fair?

Trains, planes and cars,
Increasing every day,
Why do we all use them? There's lots of other ways.

Mother Earth's alive,
And so are we,
For how much longer? Let's wait and see.

Katherine Holden (12)
Longfield School, Darlington

Bullying

B ig kids in the yard.
U nderstanding the consequences if you don't speak up.
L ooking around knowing they're coming back.
L ies are told just to hide the truth.
Y ou think the world's against you.
I n a corner crying.
N o one cares about you.
G ot to tell someone or it'll never stop.

Lauren Vitty & Lucinda Close (12)
Longfield School, Darlington

Swim, Swish

Swish, swoosh!
The waves are rippling,
Swish, swoosh!
A back is arching,
Swish, swoosh!
Pin-head eyes are searching,
Swish, swoosh!
A skinny beak is rooting.
Swish, swoosh!
She is a river dolphin,
Swish, swoosh!
She's almost extinct,
Swish, swoosh!
They're nearly gone,
Swish, swoosh!
She's trapped in a net,
Swish, swoosh!
She's gone forever,
Swish, swoosh!
Because of nets!
Stop the nets! Save the dolphins!

Lauren Wilson (11)
Longfield School, Darlington

Bullying

People get hurt, people lie.
Tell the truth then you won't have to cry
Because it will all stop
It won't go over the top.

The teachers will thank you
And also sort you out,
And will also thank you
And say, 'Well done'
Then it will stop
And you can have lots of fun!

Ashleigh Robinson (11)
Longfield School, Darlington

Pollution

Acid rain is falling,
It's all so very appalling,
Acid rain is flowing,
So the danger must be growing.

Acid rain and smelly pollution,
I think I've found the perfect solution,
Walk to school,
It's kinda cool.

Meet up with friends,
The fun never ends,
Walking is best,
But when it's dark wear a vest.

Pollution's getting bigger,
It must be pulling a trigger.
So what are you going to do?
So the trigger doesn't hit you!

Alyx Colman (11)
Longfield School, Darlington

Bullying

People get hurt when you bully them
Talk to someone and let it out,
If you don't you will get ill.

Bullying, bullying, just don't lie
Bullying, bullying just don't cry.

Bullying is sad and upsetting
So don't keep it inside
Talk to a teacher and they
Will shout at them
So let it out then go
Home and have fun, fun, fun!

Bullying, bullying just don't lie
Bullying, bullying just don't cry.

Chantelle Cooper (11)
Longfield School, Darlington

What About?

What about the animals
All the birds and bees?
They'll all be gone soon,
Help them please.

What about in Africa
With poverty and disease?
Hungry and poorly
Help them please.

So about the animals
That could die soon
Join an animal charity
Keep the world in tune.

So about in Africa
Where everyone is ill
Give money to a charity
Keep the deaths to nil!

Sophie McIntosh (12)
Longfield School, Darlington

What Happens When You Eat Meat Pie?

Don't go into the woods today,
With a gun in your hand,
Please keep away.
The animals don't need to die,
So you can have your meat pie,
If things don't change then you will find,
There will be no animals to leave behind
For children of the future to see,
Only pictures of how it used to be,
All because you wanted your meat pie,
The animals had to die,
Remember
If you are prepared to kill an animal,
Then you must be prepared to face the consequences.

Danielle Jameson (12)
Longfield School, Darlington

Save The Planet

The Earth is dying,
We must stop now,
Polluting the lovely land,
But I wonder how.

Gases are all around us,
With rising levels of carbon dioxide,
Polluting the lovely land,
Lead to flooding on the dockside.

Stop wasting energy,
We must stop now,
Polluting the lovely land,
But . . . I wonder how?

Sam Read (12)
Longfield School, Darlington

Eco Poem

I am Mother Nature, I respect this delicate world.
I make everything in it and you have to destroy it.
Why don't you respect this gift I've given you?
I try my hardest but you have to do your bit.

The animals are a big part of nature too,
But because of us they are slowly dying.
We need to help the Earth and animals
If you don't do anything there's no point in crying.

Recycle, walk and try to help us
We all have to try and turn to green
It may be hard but life is sometimes
Make your mind up or we might not be seen.

Hollie Gartland (12)
Longfield School, Darlington

Bullying

People get hurt cos you're cruel to them,
Tell the teacher and they will shout at them
Don't bully cos it's bad for you.

Bullying, bullying just don't cry,
Bullying, bullying just don't lie.
The teacher will help you,
Also sort you out.
The teacher will thank you,
Ever so much
So just go to the teacher and explain why.

Kayleigh Beckwith (11)
Longfield School, Darlington

War And Poverty

War can start from something small,
And get bigger and bigger until it's tall.
War is like a raging storm
Many lives can be nipped and torn.

Poverty is spread all over the place
Into virtually no space
People might think it's all over.

War is like an eagle's claw,
Poverty is like a closed door.

Eric Bowlby (12)
Longfield School, Darlington

Green Poem

G rowing trees and plants
R ain settling on the grass
E legant birds flying high
E nergetic winds pass
N ight sky on the fields it will lie

P eckish badgers running into a bush
O blivious foxes running around
E ven some movement in a rush
M ore rustling with a soft sound.

Sarah Fernandes (12)
Longfield School, Darlington

Do Your Part

Bath time, brush time, water still comes out.
Turn off the tap while nobody's about.
Drip, drip, drop, goes the water in your home.
A drought will appear, with one drop alone.

A drought means no water, very little, very small.
For a drink, for a bath, for nothing at all.
No water to feed your mouth, no water for your heart.
So all you have to do is your part
Be water smart!

Ashleigh McGargle (12)
Longfield School, Darlington

Litter Is Polluting The Environment

L itter is polluting the environment
I t never gets put in the bin
T ins, bottles, cardboard and food
T hrown on the floor
E very day
R emember to put it in the bin.

Emma Johnson (12)
Longfield School, Darlington

Extinction

Extinction, extinction is a terrible thing.
Extinction, extinction can be stopped by a king.

Extinction, extinction is where animals die.
Extinction, extinction some people say why?

Extinction, extinction happens to tigers and whales.
Extinction, extinction happens to females and males.

Extinction, extinction can be stopped by you.
Extinction, extinction is all down to you.

Hannah Wood (11)
Longfield School, Darlington

Recycle

R ecycle, reuse, respect
E verything you collect
C artons can be reused
Y our planet should not be abused
C ans can be turned into planes; do not let
L itter block up the drains
E verything can be recycled!

Connor Noble (12)
Longfield School, Darlington

Poem

It's always good to recycle
Instead of a car use a bicycle
Put your recyclable containers into your recycling bin,
For example, a plastic bottle, or how about a tin?
To save energy turn off all your lights.
So we can recycle without having to fight.
Recycling is great, I recycle, do you?

Emma Lyons (12)
Longfield School, Darlington

Bullying

When I get bullied I feel sick and worried.
I feel sick,
I run away quick.
My tummy is all funny
While my tears are all runny
So don't bully me or anyone else
Because if you do it is really not fun.

Danielle Willcock (12)
Longfield School, Darlington

Saving Water

Saving water can be fun.
It never works but it can be done.
Just try a little.
And do your bit.
Because saving water can be a hit.

Sophie Thomas (12)
Longfield School, Darlington

Pollution

Our world is dirty
Big and green,
It's full of water
But is it clean?
It's big, black
With puffs of smoke.
There's no clean air
It's all gone.
Our trees are green,
With hardly any air
Everyone is polluting the air.
The animals are dying black and grey,
The pond is dirty, it's not clear.

Jordan Cottnam (12)
Manor College of Technology, Hartlepool

What Have We Done?

We used to care
For everywhere
But now we hate
And it's nearly too late.

We should have known
Not to moan
To care
And to share.

We must care
For everywhere
And show
What we know.

We should have known
Not to moan
To care
And to share.

The oil will kill
The litter will fill
All the land so green
This is what I mean.

We should have known
Not to moan
To care
And to share.

Everyone help us save
Everyone love
Show love
For above.

We should have known
Not to moan
To care
And to share.

Let's work together
And save the heather
And care
For everywhere.

Kate Lawson (12)
Manor College of Technology, Hartlepool

Smoke

Smoke, smoke
Hear the needy choke
With no shelter
To stay.

Save the world
From the terror.
Save the world
And let ourselves be free.

Rain, rain,
Hear the kids in pain.
They will cry
Till they would die.

Save the world
From the terror.
Save the world
And let ourselves be free.

Holes, holes,
Filthy rubbish holes
Killing the Earth
And killing new birth.

Save the world
From the terror.
Save the world
And let ourselves free.

Daniel Pardue (11)
Manor College of Technology, Hartlepool

The World

W ar
O bey
R ule with respect
L ove people
D ie in peace.

Jemma Hagan (11)
Manor College of Technology, Hartlepool

The Whole Earth Is Looking Down

The whole Earth's
Looking down on
Our whole world
Sneezing,
Frowning
At all our wrongdoing.

Metallic birds
Try to fly.
Wings are trapped,
Fish are washed,
Together
On the ground.

The blue
Of our sky
Died yesterday
Taken by smoke -
Black and grey.

Ruined by
Its inhabitants
The Earth is dying
Who can save it?
We can save it!
The youth of today.

Lily-May Kelsey (12)
Manor College of Technology, Hartlepool

Next In Line

Knives here, knives there, knives everywhere,
People walk, people run,
But all they do is stop and stare,
Open up to *our* world and be heard,
Look up in the sky and see that bird,
Watch it fly, watch it be free,
Don't be a victim do the sensible thing,
Knives here, knives there, knives everywhere.

Jake Younger (12)
Manor College of Technology, Hartlepool

Horrible World

Earth is a home
Of different little things
We can make it better
If we work together.

Pollution is a bug
Destroying our lives
We can make it better
If we work together.

Sewers are sick
Full of green so thick
We can make it better
If we work together.

Litter on the ground
Full of cans and bottles
We can make it better
If we work together.

The day is dying, so are you
Stop and look at what we can do
Ducks are dying everywhere
Stop and look and take care.

Andrew Robinson (13)
Manor College of Technology, Hartlepool

War Is Happening!

People are dying
Guns are shooting
War is happening

Grenades are flying
People are crying
War is happening

Sky is darkening
War is finishing
War is ended!

Jodie Connolly (11)
Manor College of Technology, Hartlepool

The Environmental Scent

There once was an environment
Then it turned bad
There was a horrible scent
And that made them mad

The pollution was spreading
And the trucks were going
The world was ending
Without us knowing

The factories never stopped
There was litter on the streets
The sewage pipe got blocked
And then the pollution got beat

Recycling took over
Blue boxes full of tins
Littering destroyed the clover
And then came the green bin

The battle is won
The recycling is done
Now the environment is safe
And now there is faith.

Jordan Reynard & Alex Thompson (13)
Manor College of Technology, Hartlepool

Pollution On A Summer's Day

Lungs rotting,
Eyes clotting
On a polluted day.

Bodies dying,
Rodents trying
On a polluted day.

All this pollution, it is crucial,
On a polluted day,
Where those dead rodents lay.

Jordan Parker (14)
Manor College of Technology, Hartlepool

Our World At Stake

Have you ever wondered where your litter goes?
Your scabby cardboard boxes,
To the fungus between your toes.

Your grubby old toothbrush,
You've had since you were three,
A week-old empty sardine tin,
Your poo and even your wee,
When you throw it in the bin,
The journey shall begin.

The birds and the bees
Pray to their knees.

The rivers cry
As the animals die.
In our air there is dust,
In the sea there is crust.

The dolphins can't swim,
Their bodies are weak.

For the sanity of the Earth
Help we shall seek!

Sophie Puckrin (12)
Manor College of Technology, Hartlepool

Please Be Green

Keep the air clean,
Please be green,
Don't pollute the Earth,
The children will have had bad lungs at birth.

The world could die,
Please don't cry,
Oil is bad,
Don't be sad.

Recycle bottles of Coke,
Don't pollute the air with smoke.

Anthony Wilkins (12)
Manor College of Technology, Hartlepool

Animals And Extinction

A nimals dying
N ight-time falling
I gloos melting
M ice running for their lives
A nts scurrying around and around
L ong icy nights
S now falling

A nimals dying in the cold
N o one knows, no one cares
D eath and destruction everywhere

E verywhere you turn
X -rays and medication
T ime is limited
I gloos falling on a bear
N obody knows, nobody cares
C are is all they need
T ime is limited
I don't know what to do
O ne person is not enough
N ever leave them to die, help them, please help them.

Anna-Leigh Noon (14)
Manor College of Technology, Hartlepool

Our World

Homeless people on the streets,
Crying cars full of heat,
Breathing smoke
Up above,
Can we help them? Can we save them?

Animals dying,
Drains smelling,
People crying,
Can we help them? Can we save them?

Caitlin Stewart (11)
Manor College of Technology, Hartlepool

Recycle

Seagulls are dying
For the stuff we're buying
And throwing out again and again!
No, I'm not mad - I'm clearly sane.

The oil is killing,
No that's not thrilling,
Those animals you love so much,
Animals your children will never touch.

But there is one hope,
Recycle says the Pope
And remember be green
Not mean.

People say global warming's a myth,
But they say Obi-Wan's a Sith.
Recycle now not later,
Or you'll face the terminator.

Recycle now so the world doesn't go *boom*
Or we'll face certain doom
And thank you for listening to this.

Jack Sievert (12)
Manor College of Technology, Hartlepool

Be Green

Listen to this poem, you'll get goin'
In no time, there'll be no slime

Be green, keep Earth clean
Watch the traffic, save the Pacific

Oil sticks, don't dump it
Save the world, you'll be heard

That's the poem, now get goin'
In a day, you'll be okay.

Jonathan Umpleby (12)
Manor College of Technology, Hartlepool

Why Is The World Like This?

Pollution can do so much harm.
It can kill animals,
Also can damage the Earth
And a lot more.

Animals die because of people,
Animals live and so do people,
But you don't kill people to eat them
So why do it to animals?

Homeless children don't have a family,
They don't have a home,
They roam round the street
So just think how lucky you are.

Stabbing, why do they do it?
Do they do it for fun
Or do they do it to feel better?
So why do they do it?

Why is the world like this?
Do you believe in a better world?

Danielle Murray (11)
Manor College of Technology, Hartlepool

The World

Help the world stay the same,
Don't drop litter, you will get the blame.
Don't even try it,
We will end up living in a pit.
Keep the air nice and clean,
If you don't you are mean!
Get the point,
Go and set up a homeless joint.
So go home and sort out your tins
Into the bins.
Recycling is easy
Peasy lemon squeezy.

Ashleigh Bain (13)
Manor College of Technology, Hartlepool

World Of Darkness

Black clouds rise overhead,
Covering us in smoke.
Tornadoes of litter swirl in the wind,
Increasing in size every minute.
Oil creeps over lakes and seas,
Long arms grasp everything in its path.
The world is dying,
Fish struggle in pollution's grip.
Wings of birds are pinned down.
They are given a metallic sheen,
Overcome by black.
The world is dying,
But a new thing is coming.
One wind can bash the black away.
We can create this,
We can return colour to the world.
Go green and wipe away the black,
Don't let the world die,
Recycle!

Eleanor Gregory (12)
Manor College of Technology, Hartlepool

Pollution Will One Day Be Queen

Pollution, one day will turn our lives black,
Our world will turn invisible,
Our silky sky from its luscious blue,
To a dust filled grey,
Will one day just fade away.
Animals will swim, carefree of worries,
But chemicals dumping will catch them
And turn them with a glimmer.
Just a slight glimmer of life in their eye
Will soon turn off and out
Dance with trees, even in mother winter's wrath of cold.
Just love the world the way it is
As one day pollution may become queen.

Charlotte Welsh (13)
Manor College of Technology, Hartlepool

War

Bang there goes one
Bang there goes two
One man dies
The other comes through.

England on one side
Afghanistan the other
Both of them shooting wild
Killing one another!

Snipers on the rooftops
Machine guns on the front
Tanks are at the back
Boom! there goes another few.

Warning!
This is what will happen
Everyone will die
Leaving no one else to battle
Stop or say goodbye.

Liam Downing (13)
Manor College of Technology, Hartlepool

Don't Make A Bad World

Don't make the world so bad
As it will make the nature so sad.
Stabbing, hitting, polluting the world.
Homeless children looking for tender care.
On the floor drugs lay, in the air, chemicals stay.
Not recycling, dirty Earth hurts humans given birth.
Do you want a clean Earth?
Dead fish floating on the oily sea,
Do you know what is in your tea?
Flushing chains, washing hands, makes you a good person.
Is your Earth a healthy place?
Litter in the bin, never give in.
Make everyone smile and try not to make anyone die.
Do not do it.

Tiffany Morrill (11)
Manor College of Technology, Hartlepool

Warning - Pollution Is In The Air

Pollution is in the air,
It is everywhere.
The Earth is dying,
People are crying.
Habitats being destroyed,
Animals are starting to die.

When I fish I look out to sea
And look what I can see.
Power station polluting the air,
The sky is filled with smoke,
It makes me choke.
Fish are floating,
The sea is polluting.

People and animals living in hell,
Children and families living unwell.
Pollution, litter, global warming,
I hope this poem is not just a warning.

Craig Errington (13)
Manor College of Technology, Hartlepool

Pollution

Pollution, pollution, stop this pollution,
Make the world a better place,
By cleaning up our muck.
Help the little fish swim free.

Pollution, pollution, stop this pollution,
Make the world a better place.
Stop making the air bad.
Make people walk outside
Without them coughing their guts up.

Pollution, pollution, stop this pollution,
Make the world a better place.
Help people stop walking out into this rubbish.
Pollution is bad!

Chloe Rowbotham (11)
Manor College of Technology, Hartlepool

World War

Get your guns,
Get your spear,
War has started,
Yes it's here!

Fire your gun,
Take off his head,
The war is disgraceful,
Twenty million are dead!

Men are in battle,
Scared out of their skin,
They're here to fight,
For what they believe in!

The war is ending,
Just a few people left,
People are singing,
Britain is the best!

Robbie Brown (13)
Manor College of Technology, Hartlepool

Where Am I Going To Live?

I am on the streets,
I've got nothing to eat,
I am so cold,
Where am I going to live?

People walk past and stare,
They say look at that person over there.
What am I going to do?
Where am I going to live?

I wake up on a morning,
I am laid in black bags.
I've got nowhere to go.
Where am I going to live?
To live?
To live?

Kirsty Setchell (11)
Manor College of Technology, Hartlepool

Pollution

Pollution, it's destroying the world,
And yet we seem to continue,
So please, at least, just spread the word,
And then reframe it within you.

The Earth has become ill,
So we must care for it,
This means we must recycle,
Even just a little bit.

Stay green! And keep the world clean,
Before we make it die,
Help to destroy this disastrous scene,
Don't tell us a lie!

Admire the beauty of the world still around us,
Before it all gets destroyed,
As now the time to recycle is righteous,
So don't even try to avoid!

Adam Gilfoyle (13)
Manor College of Technology, Hartlepool

Don't Do It

Pollution is bad
I am sad
The world is coming to the end
It's driving me round the bend.
Cans go in the blue bin
Grass goes in the brown
So turn that frown upside down.
Recycling is very green
Please do not be mean.
Soon the world will blow up
That doesn't mean that you cannot recycle your cups
So you know you want to, it is cool
If you go to school.

Scott Whitmore (13)
Manor College of Technology, Hartlepool

Animals Have Gone

Look at all of the animals today
Weeping, weeping, weeping away
Now look at the animals today, left homeless
Unless we do something about it, they will be left helpless.

I mean look, at least 1,000 gone each day
Some things we may never know
Even they need a life, a risk-free life
But what's going to happen now that no one cares?

Look at all of the birds today, covered in oil
Look at all of the animals without a life
Only we can do something about it
Only we can do something special.

It's only us, the cause of all this
Only us that can save the world
I just can't see why we can't do something to save the world
All it takes is a bit of care.

Brandon Alp (12)
Manor College of Technology, Hartlepool

Untitled

Litter is falling,
Police are calling,
People are hauling,
Litter!

Litter keeps falling,
Someone stop it,
Don't you drop it!
Litter!

It has gone,
It has hit the ground,
It's all around,
Litter!

Jack Cavanagh (12)
Manor College of Technology, Hartlepool

So, It's Not You Is It?

Why do we do it?
We know what it does,
We've seen the pictures bit by bit,
We think, *that's not us!*

Little baby penguins' fur are for spoil
And are going to die.
Their little bodies cold, covered in oil,
I promise it's not a lie.

We think, *aww bless*
And we didn't do that,
But have a think, have a guess,
I wonder what you thought as you sat.

Why do *you* do it?
You know what it does.
You've heard the poem bit by bit
But you should think that *was* us.

Charlotte Grace McKenna (13)
Manor College of Technology, Hartlepool

Serving The World

All the big industrial places,
Destroying the ozone that lies in its way.
All the unsafe chemicals covering oxygen up,
The little air that is left to save the world.

This deadly environment we all live in
Is getting smaller by the second
And will be shortly coming to an end.

With cleaner chemicals
And cleaner fuels
The world will be better
For me and you!

Bethany Thornton (13)
Manor College of Technology, Hartlepool

Oh What A Wonderful World

Black smog in the sky,
Stops the birds as they fly.
Over and over and over again,
Everywhere and everywhere.

Oh what a wonderful world.

All the oil leaking,
Poor ducks, they are freaking.
Covered in an oil coat,
Came straight from that boat.

Oh what a wonderful world.

Litter piling everywhere,
Gives good people quite a scare.
All the holes are overflowing,
Who knows where the rubbish is going?

Oh what a wonderful world . . . not!

Sophie Jayne Newlove (12)
Manor College of Technology, Hartlepool

We're All The Same

People are sad,
They're all alone,
Maybe we should help,
They're just like us.

It doesn't matter if they are black or white,
Their heart is just the same as ours,
Let them join our society,
They are not terrorists, they are just citizens.

Stop the war,
Stop the abuse,
Treat them like your friends.

Robert Campbell (12)
Manor College of Technology, Hartlepool

Untitled

Litter, litter everywhere,
Pick it up and have clean air.
Homeless, nowhere to go,
Living in a tip,
Not a penny to your name,
Smelling wet and daft, day after day.
When I'm swimming in the sea
There's always fish floating beside me.
Throats are sliced, necks are broken,
Look what we have done to the world unknown.
Black people, white people, we're all the same.
Some people don't like this but who is to blame?
Black people are only tanned,
Chill out and give them a hand.
It's not their fault, it isn't ours,
Let's just forget about it,
Let's just forget about it.

Robert Bushnall (13)
Manor College of Technology, Hartlepool

Sufferers Of Terrorism

T errorists are attacking
E xplosions are happening
R ipping families apart
R espect is needed
O bjectives are peace
R etreat is impossible
I raq is a problem
S omething needs to be done
M en and women are suffering, this is terrorism.

Marcus Turnbull (14)
Manor College of Technology, Hartlepool

War Of The Worlds

War is a horrible crime,
Wounds that have to heal over time.
Blood is shed across the land,
All we need is a friendly hand.
Stop the bombs, the guns and hate,
Let's make peace before it's too late.

Finally it's coming to an end,
Soldiers march around the bend.
Crowds and bands and flags a sway,
No more tears to wipe away.
Joyful smiles from ear to ear,
Now nothing more to fear.

Let us not go back to the dreaded days,
And let them all fade away.
All the mistakes we have made,
Do not repeat the doomsday parade.

Shannon Ann Hogg (12)
Manor College of Technology, Hartlepool

No Ordinary Poem

You're probably thinking this is an ordinary recycling poem,
Well if you do think this you better get home,
Let me ask you something my friend,
Do you have a green hand to lend?
Now I know you wouldn't drop litter,
So help the dying animals get fitter,
Take a shower not a bath,
Enjoy your life, have a laugh,
Don't be cruel, follow the recycling rule!

Laura Rose Jenkins (12)
Manor College of Technology, Hartlepool

You're Not That Clever

So you think you're clever?
This won't be forever.
Everyone takes a route to the shop,
We find litter that you drop.
Stop making the world bitter
By dropping your litter.
When the bins aren't full
The world will be dull.
We know it's not all you
But you could help us too.
The animals might survive,
You're lucky you're alive.
People are dying,
Relatives are crying.
So now do you still think you're clever?
We did say it wouldn't be forever.

Kirby Raper & Stacey Bates (13)
Manor College of Technology, Hartlepool

Healing The World

People are dying all around the world
People are hungry, curled up in a box
Soldiers are saluting to their death
The world is dying with its final breath
The war is never-ending but the human life is
No one wants to make a difference
Because they're not there
If you open your eyes you'll find out war's happening
By the time you realise, we'll all be dead.

Laurence Shipley (11)
Manor College of Technology, Hartlepool

Pollution

Help the birds, the fish and the trees
Also help the bees
Stop the pollution
Solve the solution
Help all of the animals
On sea and on land
So give them a helping hand
Maybe they will make a salvation band
So stop them from polluting the world.

Lauren Taylor (12)
Manor College of Technology, Hartlepool

Pollution

P oison filling the air and sea
O ne piece of smoke kills animals
L oving families ripped apart
L ots of children homeless
U niverse is being destroyed
T oxic waste killing animals
I t is your right to save our planet
O ne little thing can change the world
N ow look after the next generation.

Tom White (11)
Manor College of Technology, Hartlepool

Reuse, Recycle

R ecycling can help us all,
E ventually all the litter will be small.
C an we all see the dangers?
Y es, now we can save what the world gave us.
C an't we all see the world is dying?
L et's save it now so it can survive.
E ventually the world can be kept alive!

Daniel Aldridge (13)
Manor College of Technology, Hartlepool

Pollution, Pollution

Pollution, pollution it's everywhere,
On the floor in your house, even in the air.
Industrial factories are not really helping,
With black smoke polluting.

Litter, litter it's all over the floor,
With it under the floor and all over your back door.
There is too much rubbish, too much mess,
Do you want rubbish to be all over your dress?

Holly Edwardes (12)
Manor College of Technology, Hartlepool

Horrible Things Happening!

People crying all alone,
Children living without a home,
People are being racist,
To people you know.
People are starving, are starving themselves to death,
People are so thirsty, they are out of breath.
We can prevent all this by looking after things.
Starting right now!

Ashleigh McCabe (11)
Manor College of Technology, Hartlepool

Animals And Cruelty

Lots of cruelty to animals in the world,
Tigers, monkeys and bears.
Thinking about it gives me nightmares.
Animals praying if only they could talk,
Some being shot and not being able to walk.
Try to help these animals in need,
Some being chained and strangled on a lead.

Josie Naylor (12)
Manor College of Technology, Hartlepool

Kill

Sewage kills, litter kills,
Where is all this coming from?

Guns kill, knives kill,
Where is all this coming from?

Elephants dying for their tusks,
Where is all this coming from?

Andrew Dennis (12)
Manor College of Technology, Hartlepool

Untitled

Families alone on the street,
Men and women that we meet.

Children getting hurt, with no home and no food to eat.
Walking around with no shoes on their feet.

Crime on the street, people getting hurt.
Let's stop this before things get worse.

Holly Jade Wainwright (13)
Manor College of Technology, Hartlepool

Our World

People homeless
Animals dead
Gases flowing
Stop all this now!

Georgia Rose Turnbull (11)
Manor College of Technology, Hartlepool

Help Us, Help The World

Stop dumping litter,
It is affecting the environment,
Put the litter in the bin
And be more eco-friendly.

Ride a bike, don't take a car,
Take a bus instead,
Be more eco-friendly
And try and save the world.

Recycle, recycle, recycle,
Recycle paper, cans and plastics,
Don't put them in the normal bin,
And be more eco-friendly.

Ride a bike, don't take a car,
Take a bus instead,
Be more eco-friendly
And try and save the world.

Deforestation is affecting us,
Even affecting the ozone layer,
Not enough trees to breathe up the gas
And be more eco-friendly.

Ride a bike, don't take a car,
Take a bus instead,
Be more eco-friendly
And try and save the world.

Animals are becoming extinct,
Because people are destroying their habitat,
Do a bit and save a creature
And be more eco-friendly.

Ride a bike, don't take a car,
Take a bus instead,
Be more eco-friendly
And try and save the world.

All you need to be more eco
Is a solar panel or wind turbine
Other things are coming soon,
And be more eco-friendly.

Ride a bike, don't take a car,
Take a bus instead,
Be more eco-friendly
And try and save the world.

Andrew White (11)
Oxclose Community School, Washington

Help The Planet

War is a bore,
Please obey the law,
Start a rhyme,
But not a crime,
Save the trees,
Help the bees.
Be very nice,
Don't melt the ice,
If you destroy,
You will very much annoy,
Save the trees,
Help the bees.
As you grow,
The rivers flow,
If you throw,
You'll never know,
Save the trees,
Help the bees.
If you be green,
We'll never be mean,
If you litter,
You'll be bitter,
Do not die,
Do not cry,
Try.

Molly Dyson (11)
Oxclose Community School, Washington

Rubbish

Save, save the environment
Save
Save the world
Save, save the little animals dying on the Earth
Stop throwing cans in the river
And stop flicking tabs on the floor
And look - a different litterbug has just entered the door.
All the animals are crying
The rainforests are dying
So save
Save the environment
Save
Save the world
Save the little animals dying on the Earth
All your chippy trays on the floor
Makes the town look horrible
So I suggest
We stop
Stop
Stop
And all join in
And put our litter in the bin.

Gareth Leadbitter (11)
Oxclose Community School, Washington

Environment

Everyone has a part in the world,
Nagging at children for making the world full of dirt,
Virtual games make the climate change,
Inside everyone cares for the world,
Reading stops you watching TV,
Once or twice you helped the world,
Making a game up *not* on the virtual world,
Everyone helps by recycling and making space,
No one has ever never helped the world,
Two or three of us do it all the time!

Zoe Brown (11)
Oxclose Community School, Washington

Animals, Poor Animals

Animals, oh poor animals
Where have you gone?
Left my sight oh precious one!
Come back to me oh furry friends.
This can't come to an end!

My poor friends have now gone
And many more will soon go,
So help everyone,
Come on gather round,
Let's lift the sound of happiness.

All I want is my animals back
And for endangered to be no more.
Come now everyone, together we can do it,
From extinction to pollution,
Let's just save the planet.

If we all work hard
My dream may come true.
Animals are dying,
It's all our fault,
Let's all try hard. I never forgot.

Judith Louise Blair (12)
Oxclose Community School, Washington

Stop!

Littering might sound cool to you, but trust me it is not
Especially when you have so much, it ends up as a lot,
Litter blows all over the ground
So you have no space to turn around.
Everybody stop, just stop, just stop,
When you find out it's pollution you will get a shock.
It's horrible when you throw rubbish around,
Because it will bounce straight off the ground.
You need to think first, before you do,
Just be sensible, yes you!
Everybody stop, just stop, just stop.

Abbie Reavley (11)
Oxclose Community School, Washington

Racism

Racism is horrible,
It's unstoppable
Unless you try,
Say goodbye to racism.
Now you know,
You get arrested
If you do.
You're not a nice person.
Report racism,
It's the right thing to do.
If it's you, say sorry to them.
If you call them black,
Your record goes into a sack.
They haven't done anything to you,
So why do something to them?
So treat them as your friends,
Then they won't kill themselves,
Because if they do kill themselves
You get arrested for life.
So report racism,
It's the right thing to do.

Ethan Eglintine (11)
Oxclose Community School, Washington

The World

The environment is crying out for help,
The world is dying without the oil,
Or is it the oil's fault?

The war is taking over,
In Iraq and Afghanistan,
We can solve this with a simple sorry.

Littering is everywhere,
Killing our world.
Stop the madness, put the rubbish in the bin.

Help save the planet by recycling.

Lewis McCartney (11)
Oxclose Community School, Washington

Save The World

The world needs to change,
It's always in a rage.
Rainforests are dying,
Animals are crying.

Littering streets is making them smelly,
Spoiling the environment are our tellies.
Recycling keeps us on our feet,
Helping the environment is neat.

The animals are gone,
Hunters are wrong.
Bring back animals and trees,
Praying on our hands and knees.

Working together,
Brings back our world forever.
Helping the environment brings pride and joy,
Having a world is a joy.

Save our world now!

Elizabeth Hope (11)
Oxclose Community School, Washington

The Environment Is Good And Bad!

The environment is good and bad.
A carbon footprint we've all had.
But there are good things, trees that sway
And snow that falls on Christmas Day.
The environment is good and bad,
Some things are good and bad
Like the rain that falls,
That makes our crops grow and not dry
And it makes the grass green.
So the environment is good and bad!

Rachael Smith (11)
Oxclose Community School, Washington

Turtles

Midnight on the shore
Of a desert island,
One thousand pearly stones lie still
In sandy coastline craters.

Crackle, crackle, crack,
The babies hatch out
Climb the sides of the hole
And amble toward the sea.

But on the way there is some danger
For the little turtles.
If they should run into a crab
Then life's at an early end.

As the first ones reach the sea,
Their long life begins,
Until they come back once more
To lay their eggs for another generation.

Daniel Joseph Bainbridge (11)
Oxclose Community School, Washington

The Environment

The environment is good and bad,
Though sometimes the weather can make me sad,
When I heard about global warming
I couldn't be bothered to wake up that morning
Because I didn't want to be there,
Some people just don't care!

In the winter when I can feel the heat
The litter is piled up on the street.
That's not right, winter should be cold,
Summer should be hot, not freezing and bold.

The animals are hibernating all around,
I can't even hear that rustling sound.
The sun is setting, it might not come back,
Because of you, you should have been recycling that!

Charlotte Falloon (11)
Oxclose Community School, Washington

Environment

As the birds begin to scutter
And the rats are in the gutter,
Pollution is everywhere,
Even in the air!

People decide to litter,
They don't think it's bitter,
The sun is getting too hot,
The ice is starting to rot!

As some plants grow tall,
The others begin to fall,
Humans are mighty and strong,
We last ever so long!

All animals have homes,
But they don't have a comb.
'They call this a habitat,'
Says the friendly tabby cat.

Laura Hodgson (12)
Oxclose Community School, Washington

Environment

The environment is dying slowly,
So stop polluting and you won't get lonely,
So be a bit green,
And don't be mean.

The ozone layer is going to die,
So stop polluting while there's time,
Save the planet,
Don't smash it with a mallet.

People should stop cutting trees,
Before there are no more leaves,
Racism is nasty,
So don't be a pasty,
Let's all join in
Throw your rubbish in the bin.

Ryan Moorhead (11)
Oxclose Community School, Washington

Animals In Extinction

There are animals in extinction, we need to stop it now.
Dolphins, monkeys, cheetahs and polar bears, penguins and whales,
Their habitats are being destroyed, we have got to stop it,
Whales and dolphins are getting wiped out by pollution
Or by getting caught.
There are animals in extinction, we need to stop it now.
The monkeys are dying fast in their rainforest homes,
The trees are getting cut down, recycle now.
There are animals in extinction, we need to stop it now.
Polar bears and penguins are dying fast,
Because the ice caps are melting in the icy tundra,
Due to the pollution around the world.
There are animals in extinction, we need to stop it now.
Cheetahs are getting shot for their soft fur,
To make fur coats or soft toys, but it's better if it's faux fur
And it will stop the cheetahs becoming extinct.
There are animals in extinction, we need to stop it now.

Kelsie Outhwaite (11)
Oxclose Community School, Washington

My Green World

M any people died in the war,
Y ou should not join, or there'll be even more.

G reen is the best colour to support,
R acism should reduce down to naught,
E co is the thing, yes we should pray,
E very single year it gets hot in May,
N ow we should help our world.

W ork hard, go straight, not in a swirl,
O ur world is the best place ever,
R iots should be a never,
L ots of things can make a difference,
D ifferences matter, so let's go and see some mince,

And that's my green world!

Caitlin Sweeney (11)
Oxclose Community School, Washington

Recycle

Our world is good, our world is bad,
Full of people either nice or mad,
But now pollution starts to flow,
Let the flowers and plants grow,
Recycle.
If this is the world coming to an end,
With homeless animals round the bend,
Before they die,
Say goodbye . . .
Or recycle!
Be green
Or be mean.
There's a lot you can do,
Before they get you.
Hurry up! Do your part!
Put your bottles in a cart,
And go and recycle!

Sophie Baker (11)
Oxclose Community School, Washington

Save The Earth

The world is not green
Because of factories letting out steam
We should all recycle
Don't take the car, ride your bicycle
Turn off the light
The monster will not bite
Global warming is going to arrive
If we keep having to drive
If you don't put your litter in the bin
A shark or fish may lose their fin
Make the planet be much better
To the government just write a letter
Now the poem has come to an end
Let's make a new start around the bend.

Francesca Christer (11)
Oxclose Community School, Washington

Save The Environment

The world is dying,
And people are crying.
It's coming to an end,
And we're taking it round the bend.
It's fading away, but we will pay.
There are many ways we can stop this.
Stop littering,
Use less fuel,
Don't use as much deodorant,
Switch off plugs
And many more.
The world is dying,
People are crying.
It's coming to an end,
And we are taking it around the bend.
It's fading away, but we will pay.

Dale Helens (12)
Oxclose Community School, Washington

Pollution

P lastic being wasted every day
O ld things could be recycled
L itter being thrown on the floor
L ong bales of rubbish going in the ground
U nderstanding people recycling
T rees being ripped down for no reason
I nconsiderate people chucking litter on the floor
O pen your eyes and see the world
N ever ever give up, help save the world today.

Luke Iley (11)
Oxclose Community School, Washington

Carbon Footprint

Can you identify where you are?
Take a look,
If you're in the garden
Or in the house,
Look around,
If there's a phone charger in the socket,
Well, unplug it!
Because you will see in years to come,
Look to see if your carbon footprint has gone!

Reece Daymond (11)
Oxclose Community School, Washington

Nature Is Beautiful

The sun shines,
The grass is green,
Roses growing on the summer rose bush,
Nature is beautiful.

Water shimmers racing the fish,
Animals graze slowly,
Trees grow tall
On the lovely day.

Jessica Kimberley Hill (11)
Oxclose Community School, Washington

Our World

Why has the world changed so much
With the forests becoming dust?
Why has the world changed so much
With the ice caps vanishing to waste?

The birds dying, life ending!
Helpless animals suffering.
What has the world become?

Sam Armstrong (13)
Queen Elizabeth High School, Hexham

What Can We Do?

What can we do?
Our Earth is dying,
Our animals are crying,
Our people are dying.

What can we do?
Pollution and climate change
Are destroying our world
Day by day.

What can we do?
We cut down the forests
In huge swathes
Leaving animals with nothing.

What can we do?
Our thirst for oil
Leaves lives ruined
And many dead.

What can we do?
Poverty, the great killer
More destructive than even war,
It plagues us.

What can we do?
The past has gone,
It's already been made,
We can't change it.

What can we do?
The future waits,
It's undecided,
We can shape it.

What can we do?
When push comes to shove
Will our politicians
Rise up to it?

What can we do?
We have the resources,
We have the means,
But can we use them for good?

What can we do?
The children of yesterday
Are the adults of today,
We've seen what happens and how to change.

What can we do?
A new generation is dawning,
We know what to do,
But is it too late?

What can we do?

Ian Shevlin (14)
Queen Elizabeth High School, Hexham

No Excuses

Endangered species,
Rainforest depletion,
Nothing to be done.

Litter, pollution,
Poverty, execution,
Nothing to be done.

Racism, war,
Pointless laws,
Nothing to be done.

After all, we're only human.

Breeding programmes,
New tree planting,
This could all be done.

Pickers, public transport
And justice,
These could all be given.

New wave thinking,
Clever governments,
These could be introduced.

After all, we are a global community.

Fiona Liddle (13)
Queen Elizabeth High School, Hexham

Death To The World! Or Life A Little Longer?

The world is dying
Though no one seems to care.
We humans are the cause,
We humans are the answer.

People say we need to stop pollution
Though no one does a thing,
So let's just belt out smoke and gas
More and more, to give all life a quicker death.

Death and destruction all around
There is no escape from pain,
I want to cry everywhere I go
Seeing the harm we have caused.

The world is dying
Though no one seems to care.
We humans are the cause,
We humans are the answer.

The rainforests are being cut down
So we can live in comfort all the time.
How evil it seems, that we kill
For comfort, despicable I feel.

Animals being edited and changed
For who? The human kind.
A two-headed kitten actually created,
But what use is that but amusement?

The world is dying
Though no one seems to care.
We humans are the cause,
We humans are the answer.

Have you ever seen a dodo?
No I didn't think so.
Know why? It's extinct
Killed off, never to be seen again.

We have to do something, don't you see
Or do you want to be responsible
For all life on Earth to die?
Will it be you or will you help the world?

Everything will die unless we stop pollution,
It's up to you.

Help! I hear all the living call, will you?

Rachel Hendy (13)
Queen Elizabeth High School, Hexham

Deforestation And The Dying World

In the beginning, there were ten candles glowing vividly -
Like the pastel colours of dawn.

The candles represent an army of people,
They are becoming weak, weaker
Until they start to flicker dangerously.
One by one they become only fiery embers,
In the eerie shadows of the nocturnal hours.

The dripping wax slides down the side of a candle,
Lives come to an end
As rainforests are destroyed.

A candle needs oxygen to burn,
A person needs it to survive.
The oxygen supply is dwindling,
As trees are smacking against the ground.

Now there is only one candle left,
What are we going to do when it goes out?

Who is going to ignite the flames once more?

Finola Fitzpatrick (13)
Queen Elizabeth High School, Hexham

As I Walked

I'm walking down the street
Without missing a beat,
Thinking how in this world we cheat
But no one seems to care
As the world tears.

A jet passes overhead
Off to the land of bloodshed.
Why do we have to fight?
Money is just getting tight.

I see a man sitting in a doorway,
For him everything is not OK.
Who knows what his story is,
I wonder if he's missed.

A group of black teens walk by,
Why is there a silent divide?
Everyone is equal,
It doesn't matter the colour of their soul.

I then think of pollution, recycling and litter,
All linked, all bitter.
I feel the sweltering heat,
Climate change can't be beat.

I think the rainforests are being killed
By cutting down trees and not being refilled.
I think of the animals becoming extinct,
Some species' population begins to sink.

My final thoughts are of the children,
Less fortunate than us,
Living in poverty, the dirt, the dust.

Our Earth is torn
But it can be reborn.
Our generation is the key
But we'll just have to wait and see.

Bryony Porter-Collard (14)
Queen Elizabeth High School, Hexham

Help!

Climate change!
Why does it happen?
Because . . .
People litter,
People fight,
People poach,
People pollute,
People have wars,
People don't recycle,
People drive,
People don't care!

The animals!
What is happening to them?
Climate change destroys . . .
The leopards,
The monkeys,
The polar bears,
The dolphins,
The birds,
The tigers' habitats,
Take action!

Help!
You need to . . .
Not litter,
Not fight,
Not poach,
Try not to pollute,
Don't have wars,
Recycle,
Drive less,
So the animals can survive
And we can save the planet!

Miriam Nohl (13)
Queen Elizabeth High School, Hexham

I See You

I see you driving your large car
Too low to be an off-road car
Too big to be a family car
As pointless as a flying plant

I see you throwing out your rubbish
Going into a landfill site
You could recycle it
But you can't be bothered to do that

I see you wasting electricity
Leaving the TV on
Your bill is going up and up
But you don't care

I see you killing the world
Wasting energy all day long
I see you
I see you

I see you.

Sam Atkinson (14)
Queen Elizabeth High School, Hexham

Pollution

Pollution is an impossible truth.
It's hard to believe,
Yet we are the ones causing it,
Our daily litter
Is killing the land,
Like a foot on a spider.

Why can't pollution be a possible lie?
We don't want to believe it,
But we are forced to.
We can't live our everyday life,
Or can we?
Why are we killing the land,
Or are we?

Megan West (13)
Queen Elizabeth High School, Hexham

No Winner

As the rich rage war, the poor people suffer.
As hate still grows, life gets tougher.
Life on the street will never be the same.
People think life is just a game.
No one will know the exact reason,
Why politicians betray people with treason.
Sending men off to war,
Terrorising them with blood and gore.
Many die with their boots on,
With a pull of a trigger they're all gone.
The sights they see on the battlefield,
If they get back their lives they won't be healed.
Another soldier passes away,
The whole world watches at the end of the day.
Families are torn apart
From soldiers dying for their country out of the good of their heart.

In war there is no winner,
All it is, is just a killer.

Ben Mole (13)
Queen Elizabeth High School, Hexham

Why?

Why are we here?
What are we doing?
Why are we doing it?
What should we be doing?
Why aren't we?

What are we here for?
Are we the only ones here?
If we are, what are our duties
And are we fulfilling them?

Why are we fighting wars?
Is killing justified ever?
Were we made for this?
I think not!

Chester Dixon (13)
Queen Elizabeth High School, Hexham

Crystal Ball - A Global Warming Story

The girl looked into the magical crystal ball,
As the crispy autumn leaves began to fall,
And the iridescent lake flowed majestically,
As the stars shone as bright as fireflies,
She saw an endless polluted sky,
Where the stars were going out,
Global warming destroying everything in its path,
Piles of rubbish rising as high as eagles soar,
The planet she once knew was no more,
Exhaust fumes whistled gleefully at the mess they helped to make,
The lush green gardens had turned to lost happiness and broken dreams,
Like pirates confused on an undiscovered stream,
One snow-white bird flew through the dusty clouds,
Like fish swimming through seaweed,
And as the girl watched the sky go black,
She knew the people destroying the world,
Had to go back.

Rhiannon Rowlands (13)
Queen Elizabeth High School, Hexham

Rainforest

The sound of trees
Hitting the rainforest floor
Rings through the silence.

The sound of chainsaws roaring
Cutting through the homes
Of innocent animals, now homeless.

Birds flapping, monkeys squealing
Running away from machines,
That'll make them homeless too.

Lumberjacks get paid to destroy
And wreak havoc in the once peaceful
Silence of the rainforest.

Joscelyn Lucas (13)
Queen Elizabeth High School, Hexham

The Grand Campaign

I have an idea
To put a smile on your face
A grand campaign
To put trees in space

I will build a shuttle
Full of all sorts of things
It will fly round the world
With its magical wings

In the greenhouse in the sky
I'll put all kinds of stuff
All the different animals
From the weak to the tough

But the government won't do it
'Cause they don't have enough money
They spent it all on tax cuts
Isn't that funny?

Stephen Rowland (13)
Queen Elizabeth High School, Hexham

Polar Ice

The white wonderland
Like frosted glass
Seeing the penguins cry.

You sit awake . . .
And just feel
The guilt that you could have helped.

The seas will fill
It's happening still
And will flood more and more.

If it carries on
The islands will be gone
And the animals will join them.

Hannah Blake (13)
Queen Elizabeth High School, Hexham

Don't Leave It On Standby

Don't leave it on standby,
Or the world will fly
And shatter up,
Not leaving a tiny cup.

Staying green,
People were keen,
Then life got in the way
Of saving another day.

Insulation in the roof,
Though really not foolproof,
Heat flowing into the sky
Though really money fluttering by.

Or we could keep it clean
And everything stunning green,
Oceans flowing where they would
And everything the way it should.

Sarah Carrington (13)
Queen Elizabeth High School, Hexham

I Am Your World

My world, my body,
I am your only world
And I will only ever be your world.
I'm degrading and dying,
You can't just put a plaster on the damage you've caused.
You all need to work together,
Put your heads together,
One step at a time towards helping me.
I'll let you think of the steps
But think
Everything you love
Going, going
Gone.

Oliver Howard (13)
Queen Elizabeth High School, Hexham

Sad Summer Days

As I gaze helplessly out the window
I see the line of traffic driving by,
Without them realising
They are destroying the planet.
Even with the window shut
I can smell the petrol-filled fumes
Ascending into the climate-changing ozone layer.
I take a look at the overflowing street
And see youths huddling together
Through the sad summer days.
I see a man dropping his rubbish
But not in the bin.
Is his life really worth the effect
It is taking on the birdlife in our world
Or the people who have to live knee-high in litter?
So next time you're tempted to drop litter or drive,
Think about the effect it will have on your grandchildren's lives.

Rach English (13)
Queen Elizabeth High School, Hexham

What A Smelly Place We Live In

All we want is a beautiful place
But instead it's like a mouldy loaf of bread
People don't care how they live
As long as they're healthy and alive

The binmen come and clean it all up
But for the world they can't leave it behind
It's stinky, it's smelly and no one likes it
So all people could recycle it.

With cans and papers from the drunks last night
Flying around like a flock of birds
As the sun rises everyone can see
What a smelly place they all live in

So what can we do to help
Tidy up our world?

Benji Makepeace (13)
Queen Elizabeth High School, Hexham

An Argentinian Success

My family is poor, no money, no home,
Think carefully when you read this poem.
As nothing but a backstreet girl,
With the desire to rule the world,
I set out to find a job, to earn,
I found one, my luck began to turn.

I was photographed and also spoke on the air,
When I moved to the city, my life was with flair,
My ambition burned and later I married,
The man who I knew a leader's qualities carried,
He became president, I tried to be vice,
But they wouldn't have it, they weren't very nice.

And just you remember, although I won,
Some aren't so lucky, something must be done.
Take interest,
Help the homeless!

Caitlin Bradshaw (14)
Queen Elizabeth High School, Hexham

We Can Stop This

What is wrong with our world?
Why are our soldiers killing needlessly?
Why are so many animals dying and endangered?
Why do we need nuclear bombs?

Pollution is killing our world.
Soldiers are only killing for oil.
Animals' homes are being destroyed so that we can move faster.
We don't need nukes, they only destroy our Earth even more.

We can stop this by stopping war.
We can stop this by resolving arguments.
We can stop this by giving up oil.
Stop this!

Richard Barnes (13)
Queen Elizabeth High School, Hexham

104

O' Green World

Would the world be better brown
Smothered in mud until it drowned?
Would the world be better blue
Until nothing but gigantic oceans grew?
Would the world be better red
Burning up until it's dead?
Would the world be better black
Covered only in tarmac?
Would the world be better yellow
With only deforestation as a fellow?
Or would the world be better green
With happiness and everything clean?

Kat Woolley (13)
Queen Elizabeth High School, Hexham

Hope, Dream, Imagine

Hope, dream, imagine.
Crazy thoughts; driving my mind insane,
Dreaming of that perfect world.
A bullet in my heart;
Reality hits me.
Guilt running through my veins,
Horror piercing my joyful spirit,
A long shrill scream escaping my lungs.
Rubber legs tumbling to the ground,
A bullet in my heart;
Reality hits me.
Hope, dream, imagine.

Josie Hart (13)
Queen Elizabeth High School, Hexham

Environment

E qually take responsibility for the problems of the Earth
N ot enough people recycle
V itally important to recycle
I mmediate response could save the world
R ich tycoons waste a lot of greenhouse gases
O zone layer has a lot of holes in it
N obody should pollute
M any people are not environmentally friendly
E conomies need to change
N ever take the Earth for granted
T oo many rubbish dumps around the world.

Alastair Harris (14)
Queen Elizabeth High School, Hexham

Recycle

Recycling is good!
We could make things different in every way,
But some people don't do this
Whereas I think they should.
A can can turn into another can!
A CD case can change into a pencil.
How is this going to happen
If everyone doesn't recycle?
Animals can be hurt if we don't recycle,
Please recycle!
You will help the world become a better place!

Laura Williamson (13)
Queen Elizabeth High School, Hexham

Pollution

He stood there looking at the derelict factory,
With endless amounts of smoke coming from the chimney.
The workers drove to work in their 4x4s as if nothing was happening.
The sound of car horns in the distance was like dogs barking at a stray cat.
As he walked down the narrow country lane an abandoned Tesco bag billowed
up in the air like a hot air balloon with a puncture.
The sound of empty drink cans rattling in the wind like a small child's toy
And one day it will all stop!

Louis Miller (13)
Queen Elizabeth High School, Hexham

Reconsider . . . Recycle!

As I walk through the park,
The rain slaps against my cheeks,
Juice bottles,
Crisp packets
And a Sugar magazine,
Feels as if they are chasing me,
As the wild wind sweeps them off the wet,
Muddy, stream-like path,
You could help,
You should recycle!

Annie Louise Stoker (13)
Queen Elizabeth High School, Hexham

Litter

Litter, litter, how it spoils our river,
I wonder why our rivers are so high.
You could help the green machine,
Get the fish back to the stream.
They could flap their fins, if it wasn't for the tins.
So, I bet you're wondering,
How can I help.
Well it's not the big things that count,
It's the little things that help.
Litter, litter, please help filter the world.

Jonathon Bell (13)
Queen Elizabeth High School, Hexham

Our Once Wonderful World

The lovely world we live in
Will never be the same again.
Our beautiful scenery
And exquisite wildlife,
Trees that are so big they scrape the sky,
Picturesque mountain ranges
With white peaks on them like ice cream on a cone.
We need to preserve our once wonderful world,
So we don't end up in a complete wasteland,
So just think, think about your actions.

Michael Budzak (13)
Queen Elizabeth High School, Hexham

Save The Homeless Race

Please help the homeless race,
All they have is a shoelace,
They end up sleeping on a wall,
Being kicked at with a ball,
They are sick of being chewed,
All they want is a bit of food,
If you give them 50p,
They can even buy a tree,
If you give them 20 pound,
They'll be sleeping sweet and sound.

Michael Adamson (13)
Queen Elizabeth High School, Hexham

Pollution Must Stop

P ollution is bad.
O rang-utans are sad.
L itter moving in the breeze.
L umberjacks cutting down the trees.
U nder the sea is growing.
T he ice caps are flowing.
I njustice is bad.
O tters are sad.
N eedless to say, it must stop.

Andrew Whittemore (14)
Queen Elizabeth High School, Hexham

The Rainforests

Trees are as tall as skyscrapers.
Brazil nut trees dominating the skyline.
Oxygen lost due to deforestation.
Rainforests are very tropical under all that green.
Orang-utans cry for help as trees fall.
Macaw parrots squawk, 'Go away. Go away.'
Animals, insects and plants' habitats are getting destroyed.
The Amazon River is winding as a snake goes through the rainforest,
Giving life and taking life as it travels.

Edward Common (13)
Queen Elizabeth High School, Hexham

Recycle To Make The Bins Happier

Along the road
Empty black bins sit like lonely buoys floating in the sea.
They stand there solitary,
Not proud and full.
This pile of rubbish stands there and pollutes.
As tall as skyscrapers,
Blocking the sun from the city.
Oh, to be a new, greener world.

Charlotte Steele (13)
Queen Elizabeth High School, Hexham

Summer Turning To Winter

The climate is changing
The world is getting hotter
The days are getting short
Summer is turning into winter
Winter is turning into summer
The ice caps are melting
Animals are dying
Polar bears are drowning.

Matthew Stewart (13)
Queen Elizabeth High School, Hexham

110

I Am A . . .

I am an iceberg, I float alone on water,
Silently melting as time goes by.
I am a droplet of acid rain, noisily falling from the polluted sky.
I am a tree, watching the world fall apart,
However I stand tall and high.
I am a carbon footprint, carelessly plodding around the Earth.
I am electricity, always being used up.
Does no one think of what I'm worth?
So we must all stand together to stop pollution, fighting, poverty
And lots more
Because we are all individuals and we have the power to score!

Sally Pitts (12)
Ripon Grammar School, Ripon

Homeless

Homeless children always cry,
Obese people walking by,
Mothers feed them what they can,
Eager for them to have a life, to be a man,
Living cold, sleeping rough,
Watching people eating, full and have had enough,
Never get a proper meal,
Smiles wishing to be real.

Evie Don (11)
Ripon Grammar School, Ripon

Litter

L itter is bad
I t makes me sad
T elly, family and friends
T o make amends
E veryone, everywhere stop throwing it down
R emember, remember clean up your town!

Emily May Croston (12)
St Edmund Arrowsmith Catholic High School, Ashton-in-Makerfield

Save The World

Save the world
For you and me.
Save the world,
A better place to be.

Save the world
For the penguins and ice.
Save the world
Because penguins are nice.

Save the world
Because animals are dying.
Save the world
Or they'll be crying.

Save the world
And don't be shy.
Save the world
So that the sun shines bright.

Save the world,
What are you gonna do?
Save the world
It's up to you.

Adam Dennis (12)
St Edmund Arrowsmith Catholic High School, Ashton-in-Makerfield

Racism Is Wrong

Black or white we're all the same,
It's all a stupid national game.
There's no such thing as race,
We are all from the same place.
There's no need to hide,
We're all the same inside.
Black or white we're all the same,
Like I said, it's a stupid game.

Caitlin Baird (12)
St Edmund Arrowsmith Catholic High School, Ashton-in-Makerfield

Poem About Global Warming

Poor little polar bears
Drowning every day
If it wasn't for global warming
They would be OK!

Cute, clever monkeys
Losing all their homes
All of them, not just one
Of all different shades and tones.

Many illegal poachers
Killing animals for trade
They do not understand
What impact they have made.

We could all help a penguin
If we each turned off a light
If we never wasted power
They'd probably be alright.

Sophie Adamson (12)
St Edmund Arrowsmith Catholic High School, Ashton-in-Makerfield

Poverty

Cold, hungry and alone,
That's what I am when I'm walking the streets,
Cold, hungry and alone.
I beg for money, food, or some fresh clothes,
Cold, hungry and alone.
I call out, say a prayer or two, but I'm still
Cold, hungry and alone.
I'm in despair at this point and I feel hopeless,
Cold, hungry and alone.
I wish I had friends, a family or people who understand
But no, I'm just
Cold, hungry and alone.

Emma Cunningham (13)
St Edmund Arrowsmith Catholic High School, Ashton-in-Makerfield

War

War, war everywhere
War, war you will not be spared
War, war it will spread
War, war it gets in your head
War, war you can die
War, war people cry
War, war you use a gun
War, war it is not fun.

Zak Astley (12)
St Edmund Arrowsmith Catholic High School, Ashton-in-Makerfield

Pollution

Our pollution is killing our Earth as we know,
As we watch our Earth crumble to dough.

Because what's happening to our world is not funny,
Different animals are being killed,
Also landfills are getting filled.

We need to stop our litter soon,
Because we can destroy our Earth and moon.

Ben Kirkpatrick (12)
St Edmund Arrowsmith Catholic High School, Ashton-in-Makerfield

The Litter Poem

Littering should not be done.
Do you think the Earth thinks it's fun?
Don't leave litter on the ground.
Come on, pick it up, don't just stand around.
Litter makes the world a disgrace.
If we pick it up it will be a better place.

Michael Leach (12)
St Edmund Arrowsmith Catholic High School, Ashton-in-Makerfield

Litter

L itter is bad, litter is mean.
I will work hard to keep things clean.
T he place will look better if everything's tidy.
T idy is the way I like to be.
E veryone should help to clean the Earth.
R ubbish should never be left on the floor.

Ryan Lightfoot (13)
St Edmund Arrowsmith Catholic High School, Ashton-in-Makerfield

The Rainforest

Oh the trees are so tall,
So big and strong,
Such a shame when they fall.
Their lives were so long,
But now they are gone.
Such a shame for the trees so tall.

Now the tree lies on the ground,
But it is here where other's lives begin.
They grow and grow till there
Is no light found on the ground
And all of this from that tree.
Yes, that tree that lies on the ground.

Now that shoot is a tree so tall,
And to think it was because of one tree's fall.
So this cycle goes on and on,
This tree is now so long,
It is time to do what each tree before has done, die and fall,
Such a shame
For all those trees so tall.

Lauren Lennox (12)
St Joseph's RC Comprehensive School, Hebburn

The Savannah

Life in the Savannah is always very loud,
Because of the animals in the air and on the ground.
Laughs and squeaks, roars and moans,
All around you animals groan.
The views are amazing everywhere you look,
Lions and hyenas and lots of wildebeest muck!

There's a crocodile in every pool,
Waiting to tear the head off an unlikely fool.
Cheetahs are racing,
While lions are chasing.
Monkeys are swinging
And birds are singing.

The Savannah is a truly amazing place!
One of nature's finest, full of grace.

Michael Jeynes (12)
St Joseph's RC Comprehensive School, Hebburn

A Tropical Adventure

A gushing sound of water,
A rustle through the trees.
The sound of little animals
Upon the soothing jungle breeze.

In the distance, I can see,
An approaching monkey crowd,
Standing tall and graceful,
Triumphant and proud.

It feels almost surreal to me,
The animals around,
The view from the horizon,
This rainforest I have found.

Grace Ennis (12)
St Joseph's RC Comprehensive School, Hebburn

What Am I?

I stand up tall,
Wherever I grow.
With my head held high,
Right up in the sky.

Now there's a breeze,
It's a bit of a sneeze.
My leaves are blowing
And somewhere it's snowing!

The wind is strong,
My will is gone
And I belong
To this environment.

Elice Clarke (12)
St Joseph's RC Comprehensive School, Hebburn

The Rainforest

In the rainforest what can I see?
Plenty of eyes all watching me,
Frogs, lizards and bats,
Two big, wild, fierce, stripy cats.

Waterfalls, heavy rain and rivers
So cold they make you shiver.
Colourful flowers and plants
So pretty they make me chant.

The trees so high
They almost touch the sky.
Night and day rolled into one,
Better take care of our rainforest before it's gone.

Thomas Giblin (12)
St Joseph's RC Comprehensive School, Hebburn

117

Snow Dream

I walked out into pure white snow
Icy hands and icy toes
The stars shone bright to lead the way
Through snow-covered trees that bend and sway
The night goes on dark and slow
With all beauty glistening in a wondrous glow
Windowpanes covered in sparkling frost
Reminds me of a beautiful thing I have lost
My heart tells me in hours this day will be past
When the night-time comes to me slowly at last
I am back in the snow so pristine and clean
Sadness shows me this was only a dream.

Rachel Freeman (13)
St Joseph's RC Comprehensive School, Hebburn

Tundra

Tundra
Snowy white
Polar bears and reindeer alike

Icy cold
The misty ice, burns to hold

Longest days
Oh how long the stretching night stays

Tundra
The white stretching wonderland.

Daniel Coutts (13)
St Joseph's RC Comprehensive School, Hebburn

Explore The Rainforest

I am walking through the rainforest one day,
When I saw a massive claw.
I hear birds singing loudly in the trees above.
Looking around I see colours and plants which I love.
I see water and fungi which is flowing and spreading everywhere.
Fruits are even growing on the trees over there.
The scenery is spectacular and wild.
I even see gibbons walking with their child.
Being here in the rainforest is a journey: you look at more and more,
It's waiting here for you, ready to explore.

Emily Hackett (12)
St Joseph's RC Comprehensive School, Hebburn

The Savannah - Haikus

Leaves spiral downwards
Falling from the withered trees
Animals wander

Lion, camouflaged
His face hidden in a bush
Still, waiting to pounce

Never-ending scene
Sunset far in the distance
Sinking downwards, slow.

Lauren Cuthbert (12)
St Joseph's RC Comprehensive School, Hebburn

In The Rainforest

Rainforest, rainforest oh so wet,
Lots of creepy-crawlies on the ground I met.

Fish in the water way down deep,
Predators search for something to eat.

Lumberjacks stay away,
The trees will lie naturally some other day.

And climate changes from time to time
And that's the end to my little rhyme.

George Dunn
St Joseph's RC Comprehensive School, Hebburn

The Savannah

Hot in day,
Cold at night,
On the savannah you will get a fright,
Because there are lions, buffalo and hippos too,
Giraffe and elephant, just to name a few.
All these creatures survive on the plains
And they all love the rain.
The savannah is a truly wonderful place,
With amazing animals and lots of space.

Matthew Stidolph (12)
St Joseph's RC Comprehensive School, Hebburn

Sun In The Sahara Poem

Lions, birds, beetles and bugs
Lie there motionless next to the buds.
Sunny, dry, windy or cloudy,
All the animals must feel drowsy.
Trees, plants, bushes and grass,
This environment is not trash.
Volcanoes, waterfalls, lakes and rivers,
When they erupt they make me shiver.

Kati-Lynne Weightman (12)
St Joseph's RC Comprehensive School, Hebburn

The Savannah

The sun shines over the African plains,
Lions running with wind through their manes.
Hippos in water splashing around,
Elephants trumpeting, what a glorious sound!
Giraffes, gazelles, monkeys and birds,
All run free on their own or in herds,
It really is a wonderful place,
And to see all this puts a smile on one's face!

Reece McLoughlin (12)
St Joseph's RC Comprehensive School, Hebburn

121

Hey! Hey! Hey!

As a normal car went
On the road that normal day,
A normal little bird went,
'Hey! Hey! Hey!
You can't drive along
Without a care you mean bloke,
'Cause your car fumes always
Make me wanna choke!'

As a normal girl went
In the woods that normal day,
A normal little squirrel went,
'Hey! Hey! Hey!
You can't drop that litter here,
That polystyrene cup,
You're spoiling the environment,
Just go and pick it up!'

As a normal boy
Left a room that normal day,
A normal little spider went,
'Hey! Hey! Hey!
You can't leave the room
With that blinding light still going,
You're wasting electricity,
The bulb might end up blowing!'

'Hey!' said the spider.
'Hey!' said the bird.
'Hey!' said the little squirrel
'Haven't you heard?
The ice caps are melting,
Fossil fuels are running low,
We've got to save the planet
There's not much time you know!

We've got to work together
If we're going to succeed,
So think of our dear planet Earth
And do a good deed.
Pick up some litter,
Turn out a light,
Protect the environment
We know you know we're right!'

Jocasta Hornsey (12)
St Joseph's RC Middle School, Hexham

It's Not Our Fault, Is It?

There's poverty in the world,
But it's not our fault.
Well, maybe it is,
Just a little bit!

There's a war in Iraq,
But it's not our fault.
Well, perhaps it is,
Just a bit!

The ice caps are melting,
But it's not our fault.
Well, possibly it is,
Quite a bit!

Rainforests are being destroyed,
But it's not our fault.
Well, probably it is,
Quite a lot!

There's pollution all around,
But it's not our fault.
Well, actually it is,
All our fault!

Rosie Mearns (12)
St Joseph's RC Middle School, Hexham

Litterbug!

Oi! Oi! Oi!
Goes the litterbug,
Walking down the street.
Does he know the damage
Of the plastic bag at his feet?

Cough! Cough! Cough!
Goes the little bird,
Who's landed on that ground.
Choking on that plastic bag
It splutters all around.

Gasp! Gasp! Gasp!
Goes the innocent fish,
Fighting for its breath.
Swallowing that plastic bag
Which drives him to his death.

Shock! Shock! Shock!
I hear you say,
As you read my verse.
Put your rubbish in the bin
Or it will make things worse.

Beth Veitch (13)
St Joseph's RC Middle School, Hexham

Life

Life is something we should treasure,
Something we should look after.
But many people take it for granted,
They abuse it by making it worse for those around them.

War is everywhere,
Poverty is just around the corner.

Our life is easy, everything is on our doorstep,
But we don't realise how hard it is for some people,
All they think about is, when will their next meal be?
Or . . . was that their last?

Lucy Willis (12)
St Joseph's RC Middle School, Hexham

124

If You Can . . .

(Inspired by 'If' by Rudyard Kipling)

If you can recycle when all around you don't,
If you can protect the wildlife while others destroy it,
If you can save electricity whilst others misuse it,
If you can try to end pollution while others add to it,
If you can help the homeless while everyone else just walks by,
If you can save the rainforests whilst others don't appreciate it,
If you can adopt an endangered animal while others kill it,
If you can give money to dying people while others waste it,
If you can dream of a better world when others dream of destruction,
If you can take the bus or walk when all around you take the car,
If you can protest to ban poverty whilst others ignore it,
If you can feed starving children whilst others think they're better,
If you can give to the less fortunate while others take it for granted,
If you can read a book, saving electricity whilst others sit and watch TV,
If you can go fishing while others dump things in the river,
If you can plant a tree when you've been on a flight, while others don't,
If you can eat organic food when all around you won't bother,
If you can reduce your carbon footprint while others make it worse,
If you can fill the kettle up to where you need when others overfill it,
If you can take a shower when others run a bath,
If you can litter-pick when everyone else doesn't bother,
If you cannot give up hope when everyone else gave up years ago,

Yours is the Earth and everything in it,
And what's more . . .
You will be a planet saver my son!

Lauren Read (13)
Teesdale School, Barnard Castle

Why?

Why do I walk for hours on end,
For contaminated, dirty water?
Yet you walk for twenty paces,
For clean and healthy water.

Why?

Why do I work for seven days a week,
For a measly wage to help my family?
Yet you have a free education,
That you still fail to appreciate.

Why?

Why do I live in a crumbling old hut,
That can barely stand the pounding rain?
Yet you live in a sturdy house,
With heating and insulation.

Why?

Why do I wear ragged old clothes,
That are made from scrap materials?
Yet you have hundreds of warm, designer clothes,
However you still ask for more.

Why?

Why do I suffer in poverty,
To die at a young, naïve age?
Yet you live in peace and luxury
And have many years to look forward to.

Ann Longstaff (13)
Teesdale School, Barnard Castle

126

Look At Our World

Look at our world
And what it beholds.
Look for the truth
As the secret unfolds.

Look at the rain
With acid inside.
Look at the poverty
Spreading far and wide.

Look at the litter
Creating a mess.
Look at the hunger
That doesn't progress.

Look at the icebergs
Melting fast.
Look at the crime
That haunts the past.

Look at the pain
That's caused by the fight.
Look at the people
Who are seeking what's right.

Look at our world
Fading away.
With all of our help
We could save it today.

Emily Collinson (13)
Teesdale School, Barnard Castle

Future Forest

F is for forest, don't let the trees fall,
O is for otters, let them build their homes so tall,
R is for remember to save our world,
E is for everyone, every boy and every girl,
S is for sea, so dark and so deep,
'T is for tomorrow, make it safe so we don't weep.

Megan Walker (11)
Teesdale School, Barnard Castle

Street Family

Family together,
Never apart,
One shared aim,
To stop one heart.

Creeping shadows,
Sticks of death,
We all know,
What comes next.

Silence broken,
Shadows fight,
Bullets fired,
In the night.

Choose your weapons,
Arm yourself,
Do bad people
Go to Hell?

Don't look back,
Don't regret.
They had it coming,
You can't quit yet.

Family together,
Playing with guns,
This sort of game,
Isn't for fun.

Caitlin Carr (11)
Teesdale School, Barnard Castle

Think

We've got to stop wasting and cutting down trees,
And start thinking about the chimpanzees.
Where would they live?
Where would they go?
You tell me 'cause I don't know.
The Earth is warming faster and faster,
Do you think it would help if we stuck on a plaster?
Think twice before you throw things away,
Could it be used another day?
Recycle things if you can, don't be a fool, be an eco-man.
The ozone layer's getting thinner,
Do you think it would help if we gave it some dinner?
Next time you moan about what's for lunch,
Spare a thought for the children who have nothing to munch.
Don't jump in your car if you could walk,
Think about the graceful sparrow hawk.
Keep our air pure and clean, don't just jump in your machine.
Get on your bike, let's do our bit,
It's good for the Earth and keeps us fit.
I hope this poem makes some sense,
And let's stop living in a pretence.

Georgia Tallentire (11)
Teesdale School, Barnard Castle

Planet Earth

P ollution is rotting the world,
L itter is making Earth so messy,
A nimals are dying fast,
N ow the ice is melting away,
E arth's forests are being cut down,
T oo many people are dying in war.

E veryone can do their bit,
A nd everyone can try their best,
R ecycling is a good start,
T oo late, it is not to save the planet,
H elp the Earth and make a difference!

James Tarn (11)
Teesdale School, Barnard Castle

Goodbye

Goodbye ice caps and polar bears,
Goodbye fish,
Goodbye penguins and seals,
Goodbye, goodbye, goodbye.

Goodbye grass and trees,
Goodbye cows and sheep,
Goodbye goats, pigs and mammals,
Goodbye meat,
Goodbye, goodbye, goodbye.

Goodbye crops and food,
Goodbye veg and fruit,
Goodbye air and oxygen,
Goodbye, goodbye, goodbye.

Goodbye sun and moon,
Goodbye world,
Goodbye world.

Ruth Ransom (11)
Teesdale School, Barnard Castle

Two Separate Worlds

You sit down at your PC,
I sit alone helplessly.

You eat your pizza and your chips,
I put nothing to my lips.

You go to get an education,
I do my family's food preparation.

You go to buy shoes and hats,
I sit and sew socks and mats.

You go to sleep in your comfy bed,
But my family aren't sufficiently fed.

You don't think about my loss,
Both our worlds will never cross.

Tara Evans (13)
Teesdale School, Barnard Castle

130

The World

There are people in the streets
Who live in cardboard boxes.
Some people who pollute the world
Pretend they don't know what the cause is.
There is so much pollution
There isn't really a solution.
Sometimes we feel guilt,
Knowing what we have done has made ice caps melt.
People should try recycling,
Rather than driving, go cycling.
Some people think it's OK to litter
Even though it just makes me feel bitter.
All of this makes me feel down,
Knowing that if we keep doing this we'll drown.

Elliot Rundle (11)
Teesdale School, Barnard Castle

The World Needs Help Helping People

Gangs are tough,
They think they're cool,
They don't realise that they are fools.

The world is a mess,
We need to be green,
Nobody realises that we are being mean.

What about Africans?
They have no homes,
We need to donate money to fix up their bones.

The world is a mess,
We need to be green,
Nobody realises that we are being mean.

Jack Mattison (11)
Teesdale School, Barnard Castle

131

Let's Take Action Now

Hello, how are you today?
Did you hear the news this morning?
The Earth is in need of some help.
We hear about pollution
But what's the solution?
We hear about rainforests being cut down,
Litter and drought.
Harming trees, harming wildlife,
Let's take action now.
Help save the planet, it's in the greatest need,
You can do your bit, recycle glass, paper and plastic.
Don't drop litter and switch off lights.
Let's take action now.

Sally Watson (11)
Teesdale School, Barnard Castle

Green Planet

You want animals,
Do not build on my habitat,
Keep me alive now.

P ollution - that's what you give me,
L ots and lots of pollution.
A bottle you could recycle to help me.
N ature is dying so don't make me suffer, watching them die.
E ven if you don't want to, please help me,
T rust me, it's happening now.

You should recycle now.
Litter you should get rid of.
You should recycle now.

Megan Cooper & Emma Wright (11)
Teesdale School, Barnard Castle

Eco-Lectric

Electric, electric,
It makes us in a mess.
Electric, electric,
It puts us in distress.
Electric, electric,
Turn it off at times.
Electric, electric,
It does not stop crimes.
Electric, electric,
We think it's all a sin.
Electric, electric,
We should put it in the bin.

Thomas Howe (11)
Teesdale School, Barnard Castle

Stop And Save The Planet!

She gave us all these things,
We threw them away one by one,
The beautiful rainforests are dying,
Endangered animals becoming fewer,
Can't you see what's happening to
The tiger, the giant panda and the golden lion Tamarind?
If you want to bring this to a stop
All you need to do is be kinder to our Earth.
Recycle, don't litter and don't destroy our planet.
It's the only one we've got so . . .
We've gotta look after it!

Neive Emma Percival (11)
Teesdale School, Barnard Castle

How To Be A Rainforest Warrior!

R eally rocking rainforests
A re needed for the planet,
I ncluding local tribes.
N ow if we get our act together,
F ind a different source of wood,
O ld timber's just as good.
R ight let's make a start,
E veryone find out where your furniture comes from,
S ourced from managed woods or raided from rainforests?
T ogether we can make a difference.
S ave the rainforests, don't let our planet die.

Cicely Cox (11)
Teesdale School, Barnard Castle

Do Your Bit

To help the environment it's really not that hard,
Save an animal and keep it in your backyard,
Of course you'll have to feed it regularly,
Or make the decision to set it free.
You could stop litter by setting up recycling bins,
Separate them into groups, plastic bottles, paper bags
And baked bean tins.
You could stop poverty by giving poor people on the streets 50p,
To allow them to be able to buy a decent drink,
A nice warm cup of tea.

Thomas Wilson (11)
Teesdale School, Barnard Castle

War

Loss of family, loss of friends,
Scary for families, scary for friends,
Death to family, death to friends,
Shot of bullet, drop of bomb,
Bullet to body, bomb to town,
Death to a person, death to people,
People die,
People cry,
People fight,
Would you?

Joe Reece Hutchinson (11)
Teesdale School, Barnard Castle

Save The Future

L andfills all over the world,
A nimals becoming extinct,
N on-renewable fuels being wasted,
D isaster is looming I think,
F orests can be replanted,
I ngenuity could solve our problems,
L earn to preserve our resources,
L ive a sustainable lifestyle.

Ben Lees (11)
Teesdale School, Barnard Castle

Think!

R ubbish and litter
E verywhere on the floor
C an't recycling be a law?
Y ou can see all the mess
C ome on reuse before the stress
L oads of bins overflowing
E nd the mess it's easier than you *think!*

Bethany Vasey (11)
Teesdale School, Barnard Castle

Recycling

R ecycling is great for the world
E veryone should try to recycle
C are for the world
Y ou can make a big difference
C aring can change the world forever
L eaving things is careless, so recycle
E njoy the world and recycle.

Hayley Dixon, Emma Walker & Beth Howson (11)
Teesdale School, Barnard Castle

Cycling

C ycling is so much fun and really great.
Y ou could even save the planet.
C ut down on car fumes and stop smoking problems
L ike acid rain, killing lovely trees.
I do it, now it's your turn to get on your bike.
N ow global warming is a crisis,
G ive your bit to save the planet.

Alex Harris (11)
Teesdale School, Barnard Castle

Why War?

Why are there wars?
Aren't there laws?
Fighting
With all their might.

Why are there wars?
Aren't there laws?
No one should suffer
Even if you're tougher.

Why are there wars?
Aren't there laws?
My wish
Has gone a miss
Because no one will listen
But I wish wars would stop.

Why are there wars?
Aren't there laws?
The dying,
People crying
And it's all the fault
Of one battling person.

Hannah Woodward (11)
Whitburn CE School, Whitburn

Young Writers Information

We hope you have enjoyed reading this book - and that you will continue to enjoy it in the coming years.

If you like reading and writing poetry drop us a line, or give us a call, and we'll send you a free information pack.

Alternatively if you would like to order further copies of this book or any of our other titles, then please give us a call or log onto our website at www.youngwriters.co.uk

Young Writers Information
Remus House
Coltsfoot Drive
Peterborough
PE2 9JX
(01733) 890066